T0146875

Unique Bible Quizzes

Unique Bible Quizzes

75 Thought Provoking Bible Stumpers

Pastor Willis Schwichtenberg

UNIQUE BIBLE QUIZZES
75 THOUGHT PROVOKING BIBLE STUMPERS

iUniverse books may be ordered through booksellers or by contacting:

iUniverse
1663 Liberty Drive
Bloomington, IN 47403
www.iuniverse.com
844-349-9409

ISBN: 978-1-5320-0352-3 (sc)
ISBN: 978-1-5320-0351-6 (e)

Print information available on the last page.

iUniverse rev. date: 03/28/2024

Contents

Action People in the Old Testament

(The Bible is filled with people of action—people who, under God's guidance, were busy doing things. Using the list below, name the person being described in the brief action clue. For more help, consult the Bible passage listed.)

Abraham	Daniel	David	Deborah	Elijah
Enoch	Hannah	Isaac	Jacob	Jonah
Joseph	Joshua	Moses	Nehemiah	Noah
Ruth	Samson	Samuel	Sarah	Solomon

1. He BUILT an ark (Genesis 6:13-14). _____
2. She DEDICATED her son (I Samuel 1:20, 28).
   _____

3. He LED the people into the Promised Land (Joshua 1:1-2).
   _____

4. He PREACHED at Nineveh (Jonah 3:3).
   _____

5. He BUILT the Temple (I Kings 8:51).
   _____

6. She JUDGED the people (Judges 4:4).
   _____

7. He WALKED with God (Genesis 5:24).
   _____

8. He LED the people through the Red Sea (Exodus 14:27-29).
   _____

9. She BORE Abram a son (Genesis 21:3).
   _____

10. He ANOINTED David (I Samuel 16:13).
    _____

11. He DREAMED of a "ladder" to heaven (Genesis 28:12).

_____

12. He PRAYED about Sodom and Gomorrah (Genesis 18:23-33).

_____

13. He MARRIED Rebekah (Genesis 24:67).

_____

14. He RODE a chariot to heaven (II Kings 2:11).

_____

15. He REBUILT the walls of Jerusalem (Nehemiah 1:1, 2:20).

_____

16. He BROUGHT the ark to Jerusalem (II Samuel 6:17).

_____

17. He DESTROYED a building all by himself (Judges 16:30).

_____

18. He SPENT the night with lions (Daniel 6:16).

_____

19. He INTERPRETED Pharaoh's dreams (Genesis 41:25).

_____

20. She BEFRIENDED her mother in law (Ruth 1:11, 14).

_____

ANSWERS: *(1) Noah, (2) Hannah, (3) Joshua, (4) Jonah, (5) Solomon, (6) Deborah, (7) Enoch, (8) Moses, (9) Sarah, (10) Samuel, (11) Jacob, (12) Abraham, (13) Isaac, (14) Elijah, (15) Nehemiah, (16) David, (17) Solomon, (18) Daniel, (19) Joseph, (20) Ruth.*

SCORING: 20 or 19 correct: You are a person of action when it comes to this quiz; 18 or 17 correct: We are amazed at your answers; 16 or fewer correct: More action needed in your Bible studies!

Angels in the Bible

(Only a handful of angels (three—Gabriel and Michael and Satan, a fallen angel) are given specific names in the Bible but angels "appear" often and especially when God's plan of salvation is leaping forward. Angels are not humans and they are not "gods" and humans beings were not, are not, and do not become angels. September 29 is designated in the church as the day of "St. Michael and All Angels." Technically, Michael was an angel and not a saint. However, we can still learn much about these angelic beings who served God in unique ways. Why not try this Bible quiz to identify some of the angels that walk the pages of the Bible.)

1. When Adam and Eve were expelled from the Garden of Eden I was placed at its entryway and held a flaming sword to "guard" the Garden. What was I called? (Genesis 3:24) (a) Protector, (b) Cherubim, (c) Gatekeeper, (d) Harbinger.

2. Three of us appeared to an early patriarch by the oaks of Mamre and discussed his future. We were not called angels though it is obvious that we were sent by the Lord. Who did we meet with? (Genesis 18:1ff.) (a) Noah, (b) Shem, (c) Abraham, (d) Joseph.

3. We were two of the three angelic beings that are described in the previous question. We are called angels in the Bible and journeyed to the cities of Sodom and Gomorrah to help and rescue this man and his family. What was his name? (Genesis 19:1-3) (a) Joseph, (b) Tubal-Cain, (c) Ishmael, (d) Lot.

4. I had this dream about a ladder reaching from earth to heaven with heaven at the top and I "saw" in this dream angels of God ascending and descending on it. What a dream and what a promise God gave me! Who am I? (Genesis 28:10-12) (a) Jacob, (b) Abraham, (c) Isaac, (d) Joseph.

5. Though I was not called an "angel" I wrestled with a man named Jacob and ended up causing his hip to be out of joint. He would not let me go until I blessed him and I blessed him indeed and gave him a new name. What was that name? (Genesis 32:22-28) (a) Peniel, (b) Israel, (c) Ebenezer, (d) Esau.

6. My name is Isaiah and I saw an unusual vision of angels called "seraphim" in the Temple. My question to consider is "What was very unusual about my vision of angels?" (Isaiah 6:1-7) (a) They each had six wings, (b) They were calling to each other, "Holy, Holy, Holy", (c) The place was filled with smoke, (d) One of them put a burning coal in Isaiah's mouth, (e) All of the above.

7. I was amazed that God's servants Shadrach, Meshach and Abednego were rescued from my fiery furnace by an angel. In response, I warned people about speaking against their God but I never really came to this faith. What is my name? (Daniel 3:28) (a) Belshazzar, (b) Nebuchadnezzar, (c) Darius, (d) Michael

8. My name is Daniel and I was rescued in a unique way by an angel of God. Can you tell how I was rescued? (Daniel 6:19-22) (a) God sent a whale to swallow and protect me, (b) God shut the mouth of lions and they could not attack me, (c) God carried me away to Babylon where I was free from attacking beasts, (d) God sent a flood to drown my adversaries.

9. We are angels and the life and ministry of Jesus was affirmed again and again by us angels. We were present at all of these times "except" for (a) The birth of Jesus, (b) Jesus' temptation, (c) Jesus praying in the Garden of Gethsemane, (d) The time Jesus was on the cross, (e) The tomb of Jesus after the Resurrection.

10. My name is Jesus and when I was being arrested in the Garden of Gethsemane my impetuous disciple, Simon Peter, tried to help me and ended up cutting off someone's ear. I admonished him and said that if I wanted and

needed to, I could have angels help me. How many angels did I say I could summon from my heavenly Father? (Matthew 26:53) (a) Seven, (b) Ten, (c) Twelve legions, (d) Fifty Thousand.

11. When Jesus ascended into heaven I told the disciples that Jesus would come back in the same way that they were seeing him go. I used the following words to address the disciples. (Acts 1:11) I called them (a) Men of Galilee, (b) Men of Jerusalem, (c) People of God, (d) Fellow servants of the Lord, (e) You disciples of Jesus.

12. While I was travelling from Jerusalem an angel appeared to me and told me to go to Gaza and to meet a man from Ethiopia who was studying Scripture. I was sent to help him. What is my name? (Acts 8:26) (a) Simon Peter, (b) Paul, (c) John, (d) Philip.

13. One day I put on my royal robes to make a speech to the people. Everyone was so impressed with what I said, they cried out, "The voice of a god and not of a man." I smiled and accepted this accolade but an angel of the Lord struck me down with a terrible illness and I was filled with worms. What is my name? (Acts 12:20-23) (a) Caesar, (b) Festus, (c) Herod, (d) Pontius Pilate

14. It's difficult keeping people in prison when they have angels on their side. I addressed a group of Sadducees who did not believe in the resurrection and together we had some of the disciples arrested but an angel opened the prison doors in the night and had them released. Strangely enough, they were back in the Temple the next day preaching about Jesus. Who am I? (Acts 5:17-21) (a) Pontius Pilate, (b) King Herod, (c) Gamaliel, (d) High Priest

15. I am the unknown author of the book of Hebrews and I wrote about "entertaining" angels when a person is not aware of it. Which Old Testament couple "entertained angels" without knowing for sure that they were angels?

(Hebrews 13:2) (a) Adam and Eve, (b) Noah and his wife, (c) Abraham and Sarah, (d) Moses and Zipporah.

ANSWERS*: (1) b-Cherubim, (2) c-Abraham, (3) d-Lot, (4) a-Jacob, (5) b-Israel, (6) e-all of the above, (7) b-Nebuchadnezzar, (8) b-God shut the mouth of lions and they could not attack me, (9) d-The time when Jesus was on the cross, (10) c-Twelve legions, (11) a-Men of Galilee, (12) d-Philip, (13) c-Herod, (14) d-High priest, (15) c-Abraham and Sarah.*

SCORING: If you had 14 or 15 correct you know much about these heavenly beings; if you had 12 or 13 correct you have learned much about these heavenly beings; if you had 11 or fewer correct you, like all of us, have much to learn about these heavenly beings.

Animals in the Bible

(The Bible is filled with animal imagery and information about animals. More than 50 are mentioned in the Bible. Name the animals suggested by the clues. Check the Bible reference if you need help.)

1. This animal returned to Noah's ark with a leaf in its beak. *(Genesis 8:11)*
2. This animal was considered unclean by the Hebrews, but in the New Testament Peter was told in a dream that he should "eat" because it was no longer unclean. *(Acts 10:12-15)*
3. These sea "animals" were the basis for a large meal in the New Testament even though the serving portions were probably fairly small. *(Matthew 14:19-21)*
4. This animal is mentioned in the Psalms but it was also curled around the Tree of the Knowledge of Good and Evil in the Garden of Eden. *(Psalm 91:13)*
5. This sea "animal" had one of God's prophets for lunch, but, by God's grace, the meal did not agree with it three days later. *(Jonah 1:17)*
6. This docile animal is the basis for much imagery in the Bible and is also a symbol of the Messiah. *(Isaiah 65:25)*
7. This mythical one-horned animal is mentioned in the King James Version of the Bible. *(Job 39:9-10)*
8. In an unusual Old Testament account a female of this species destroys some children in a village. *(II Kings 2:23-25)*
9. These animals were worshiped by the Egyptians but when they began to hop around in hordes, the Pharaoh cried "Uncle!" *(Exodus 8:5-6)*
10. This animal was allowed to "escape" on the Day of Atonement and this act became symbolic of our sins being

placed on the head of someone else, the Christ. *(Leviticus 16:-10)*

11. This is the only talking animal ever mentioned in the Bible. *(Numbers 22:30)*

12. Samson and David both killed one of these vicious animals. *(I Samuel 17:34)*

13. This modern day pet was generally a wild animal in the Bible and in one story even licked the leprous sores of an individual. *(Luke 16:21)*

14. Jesus urged us to exemplify these winged animals who don't seem to worry about the future. *(Matthew 10:29)*

15. These animals are symbolic of those in the world who teach false doctrine. *(Matthew 7:15)*

ANSWERS: *(1) Dove, (2) Swine or Unclean 4 footed beasts; (3) Fish, (4) Serpent, (5) Great fish or whale, (6) Lamb (Sheep), (7) Unicorn, (8) Bear or She-Bear, (9) Frogs, (10) Goat or Scapegoat, (11) Donkey, (12) Lion, (13) Dog, (14) Sparrows (birds), (15) wolves*

SCORING: 15 correct: You know the birds of the air and the fish of the sea; 14 or 13 correct: You kept moving across the face of the page; 12 or 11 correct: No animals were harmed in the taking of this quiz; 10 or fewer correct: Join Adam in naming the animals.

Annual Meetings in the Bible

(At the beginning of the year many congregations have their Annual meetings, a time to gather and reflect on goals, ideas, accomplishments and mission and ministry in general. A few such meetings are mentioned in the Bible. See if you can determine the answers to "Annual Meetings in the Bible" without checking the Biblical reference.)

1. In a holy "meeting" in eternity the Triune God considered making humans in His image and decided they would (Genesis 1:26) (a) rule over the fish of the sea, (b) rule over the birds of the air, (c) rule over the livestock, (d) rule over all creatures, (e) all of the above, (f) none of the above.
2. God had a surprise meeting with this individual concerning a righteous man from Uz who was very wealthy and successful (Job 1:6-12). Whom did God meet with? (a) Job, (b) Abraham, (c) Ezekiel, (d) Satan.
3. Three "godly" visitors met with Abraham in the Old Testament near Mamre (Genesis 18:16-32) and revealed their promise of giving him a son but also warned (a) that Sarah would die in childbirth, (b) that Lot was going to get the better property, (c) that Sodom and Gomorrah would be destroyed, (d) the Tabernacle would be "lost."
4. When Moses met with God, He saw God in the form of (a) a pillar of fire by day, (b) an angel with said his name was Gabriel, (c) the Angel of death wielding a sword, (d) a voice speaking from a burning bush.
5. When Boaz wanted to marry Ruth a "meeting" was called (Ruth 4) and (a) he had to redeem a parcel of land (b) the seller had to take off a sandal and give it to the other person, (c) he had to honor Ruth's mother-in-law, Naomi, (d) he had to honor Ruth's dead husband who originally owned the land, (e) all of the above.

6. Jeremiah did not attend a meeting with the King in the Temple because he was not allowed in, but at the meeting the King cut the scroll into pieces and burned it as Jeremiah's secretary, Baruch, was reading it. Name the king. (Jeremiah 36:1-26) (a) Josiah, (b) Jehoiakim, (c) Zedekiah, (d) Nebuchadnezzar.

7. At the birth of his son, no one would believe Elizabeth about their child's name so at a meeting her husband, Zechariah, ended up writing on a tablet, (Luke 2:62-66) (a) "His name is John", (b) "His name is Zechariah," (c) "His name is "Jesus", (d) "His name is James."

8. Herod met with his advisors and told these people that according to Scripture, the Christ was to be born in Bethlehem. (Matthew 2:1-2, 9-10). Name these people from the East who met with Herod. (a) Caesar Augustus, (b) Magi, (c) Augsburg Group, (d) Bonarges.

9. In a meeting, this group, led by Caiaphas, the High Priest, heard the charges against Jesus and condemned Him to death (Matthew 26:57-60, 66-68). Name this group: (a) Church Council, (b) Voter's Assembly, (c) Sanhedrin, (d) Diaspora.

10. The Early Church met together in council in Jerusalem and heard reports from Paul and Barnabas and Simon Peter and cleared up misunderstandings about rules and regulations. *(Acts 15:1-21)* Who was in charge of this meeting? (a) James, the brother of Jesus, (b) Simon Peter, the Rock, (c) Saul, also known as Paul, (d) Barnabas, the one who was the "encourager."

ANSWERS: *(1) e-all of the above, (2) d-Satan, (3) c-that Sodom and Gomorrah would be destroyed, (4) d-a voice speaking from a burning* *bush, (5) e-all of the above, (6) b-Jehoiakim, (7) a-"His name is John", (8) b-Magi, (9) c-Sanhedrin, (10) a-James, the brother of Jesus.*

SCORING: 10 correct – You are ready for your Annual meeting, 9 correct – You know what's going on; 8 correct – You need to study a little more; 7 correct – Hopefully, they won't meet without you!

Ashes in the Bible

(Ash Wednesday is the beginning of a 40 day journey called the season of Lent, leading to Easter Sunday. Technically, the Sundays in this six week observance are not "counted" in this observance because they are still considered celebrations of the Resurrection of Jesus Christ. With "Ash" Wednesday we would ask, how much do you know about "ashes" in the Bible? Consider taking this quiz as part of a personal Lenten observance and spiritual "walk." Check the Biblical reference if you need more help. If you fail, we won't ask you to repent in sackcloth and ashes!)

1. I am one of the Biblical patriarchs and when praying to God about the people in a wicked city I referred to myself as "nothing but dust and ashes." (Genesis 18:27) Who am I? (a) Adam, (b) Abraham, (c) Noah, (d) Isaac, (e) Jacob.

2. As the leader of God's people, I, Moses followed the instruction of God and tossed ashes into the air (Exodus 9:8) and these started the plague of (a) flies, (b) hail, (c) boils, (d) cattle murrain.

3. My name is Tamar and I was raped by my half-brother and in mourning this act I put ashes on my head (II Samuel 13:19). We were both children of David. My full brother, who later usurped our father's kingship, was so angry that he killed the man who did this. (II Samuel 13:32-33) What was the name of my avenging brother? (a) Absalom, (b) Ammon, (c) Joab, (d) Solomon, (e) Adonijah

4. My daughter, Esther, was the wife of the king of Persia and when I learned of a terrible plot against our people I "put on sackcloth and ashes to mourn this plot and to get my daughter's attention (Esther 4:1). Who am I? (a) Haman, (b) Xerxes, (c) Bigtha, (d) Mordecai, (e) Solomon.

5. My name is Job and I found myself mourning in ashes the loss of wealth, children, and health. My Lord God had spoken with this personal being as part of a test of my

faith and devotion. Who did God talk to about me? (Job 2:7-8) (a) Uz, (b) Satan, (c) Eliphaz, (d) Bildad, (e) Zophar.

6. In Psalm 102, the prayer of an afflicted man, I appealed to God for help and in this mourning I said (Psalm 102:9) (a) ashes are a good thing, (b) I eat ashes as my food, (c) I use ashes to make my soap, (d) my bed is made of ashes, (e) none of the above.

7. In my book of prophecy, I, Isaiah, wrote concerning the "year of the Lord's favor" that God would (Isaiah 61:3) (a) provide for those who grieve, (b) bestow a crown of beauty instead of ashes, (c) provide oil of gladness instead of mourning, (d) give a garment of praise instead of a spirit of despair, (e) all of the above.

8. My name is Jeremiah and I wrote about the place where dead bodies and ashes are thrown. I wrote that the "days are coming" (Jeremiah 31:40) (a) when this will be a holy place, (b) when this will never be uprooted, (c) when this will never be demolished, (d) all of the above.

9. My name is Daniel and under the reign of Darius, the son of Xerxes I learned of the desolation of my city and country and people and it caused me to pray with fasting, sackcloth and ashes (Daniel 9:3). Can you guess what made me so sad? (a) 70 years of desolation, (b) the end of the Davidic reign, (c) the destruction of the Ark of the Covenant, (d) the destruction of Sodom and Gomorrah.

10. My name is Jonah, the reluctant prophet. I was told by God to preach repentance to the city of Nineveh. Guess what happened (Jonah 3:6). (a) the people continued their sinful ways, (b) the people threw me in the sea where I was swallowed by a whale or great fish, (c) the people, starting with the king, repented in sack cloth and ashes, (d) God destroyed the unrepentant city.

11. My name is Jesus and when I saw the lack of repentance in the cities of my day I said that the some of the ancient cities would have repented in "sackcloth and ashes" (Matthew 11:21) if they had seen my miracles. In my discourse these

cities included (a) Tarsus, (b) Sodom and Gomorrah, (c) Bethlehem, (d) Jerusalem, (e) Caesarea.

12. The unknown writer of the book of Hebrews mentions the ashes of this animal as part of the ceremony of making people clean (Hebrews 9:13): (a) Doves, (b) crow, (c) pigeon, (d) Heifer, (e) sheep.

ANSWERS: *(1) b-Abraham, (2) c-boils, (3) a-Absalom, (4) d-Morcedai, (5) b-Satan, (6) b-I eat ashes as my food, (7) e-all of the above, (8) d-all of the above, (9) a-70 years of desolation, (10) c-the people, starting with the king, repented in sackcloth and ashes, (11) b-Sodom and Gomorrah, (12) d-Heifer.*

SCORING: 12 correct – You may not need to repent in sackcloth and ashes about your score; 10-11 correct – You are ready for Lent, 9 correct – You have a burning desire to learn more, 8 or fewer correct – Don't give up studying the Scripture for Lent!

Babies in the Bible

(The birth of children in the Bible is always a special event. See if you can determine the Biblical "babies" being described in the clues given. If you need help, check the Bible reference.)

POSSIBLE BABY NAMES *(not all will be used)*: Abel, Cain, Esau, Gomer, Isaac, Ishmael, Jacob, Jesus, John, Judah, Moses, Reuben, Samson, Seth, Solomon

1. I was the first baby born in the Bible. What's my name? (Genesis 4:1)
2. My brother was murdered by my older brother and in a way I became a "replacement" baby as the murderer had to leave. Who am I? (Genesis 4:25)
3. My father was named Abraham and I was a baby born to my father's wife's maidservant. Who am I? (Genesis 16:15)
4. My parents were pretty old when I was born as a baby. That happened several times in the Bible but my mother's name was Sarah. Who am I? (Genesis 21:1-3)
5. I was a twin baby who was often tricked by my slightly younger brother. One trick involved red stew and that color is symbolic of my name. Who am I? (Genesis 25:24-26)
6. I was the first baby born to Jacob and I ended up with eleven brothers. Who am I? (Genesis 29:31)
7. When I was a baby my mother hid me in a basket in the Nile River. Who am I? (Exodus 2:1-10)
8. When I was born my Old Testament parents were told that my hair should not be cut and that was a symbol of my incredible strength. Who am I? (Judges 13:4-5, 24)
9. My older baby brother from my mother died and I was born next and became a man of peace who authorized

the building of the Temple in Jerusalem. Who am I? (II Samuel 12:24)

10. As a prophet, I was told to have a baby with a harlot. His name is obscure and the Bible book bears my name. However, what was my wife's somewhat strange name? (Hosea 1:2-3)

11. My father's friends want to name me Zechariah but my speechless father wrote what my baby name should be. What is my name? (Luke 1:63)

12. I was a baby born in Bethlehem to a virgin mother and I was sometimes called the "Son of Man." Who am I? (Luke 2:21)

ANSWERS: *(1) Cain, (2) Seth, (3) Ishmael, (4) Isaac, (5) Esau, (6) Reuben, (7) Moses, (8) Samson, (9) Solomon, (10) Gomer, (11) John, (12) Jesus*

SCORING: 12 correct – You know your cute "baby faces"!; 11 correct – Your answers are not child's play; 10 correct – Oh, baby, not too bad!; 9 or fewer correct – Perhaps you need to study more baby names.

Birds in the Bible

(Some associate doves with Christmas. In actuality, doves are not mentioned in the Christmas story. In fact, no animals are mentioned. However, even though birds are not part of the story we rejoice in the presence of birds in the pages of the Bible. See if you can determine the bird or situation about birds being described. Use the Bible clue if you need help. The Bible book is not mentioned in the clue if it would give away the answer.)

1. As the flood waters continued I released birds four times to "test the waters" including both a raven and a dove. Who am I? (Genesis 8:6-12) (a) Noah, (b) Shem, (c) Ham, (d) Japheth.

2. I made a special sacrifice to God in honor of the covenant we made but I had to ward off winged carrion (birds of prey) which tried to devour the sacrifice. Who am I? (Genesis 15:10-11) (a) Noah, (b) Abraham, (c) Isaac, (d) Jacob.

3. I was the leader who took care of God's people in the desert, including the time when God sent quail to feed them, despite their grumbling. Who am I? (Exodus 16:9-13) (a) Abraham, (b) Isaac, (c) Jacob, (d) Moses.

4. I was fed in the wilderness with meat and bread by ravens. Who am I? (I Kings 17:6) (a) Elijah, (b) Elisha, (c) Abraham, (d) David, (e) Jesus.

5. Which of us are not described as having wings in the Bible? (Psalm 17:8, Psalm 61:4, Isaiah 6:2, Malachi 4:2). (a) Eagles, (b) God, (c) Angels, (d) None of the above.

6. The Bible has many references to eagles. Which Old Testament prophet speaks about the flying creature has the face of an eagle as well as three other faces? (1:10) (a) Isaiah, (b) Jeremiah, (c) Ezekiel, (d) Daniel.

7. My name means "dove" and some suggest that I was to bring God's peace to a rebellious nation. I ran "the other

way" on a boat until God intervened. Who am I? (a) Noah, (b) Abraham, (c) Solomon, (d) Jonah.

8. God cares for these birds so much that they do not fall to the ground without Him being aware. What bird is this? (Matthew 10:29) (a) sparrow, (b) dove, (c) pigeon, (d) stork.

9. We dedicated our child to the Lord and used the required two turtle doves in this act of worship. Who are we? (Luke 2:24) (a) Zechariah and Elizabeth, (b) David and Bathsheba, (c) Mary and Joseph, (d) Jacob and Rachel, (e) Solomon and the Queen of Sheba.

10. My name is Jesus and I told about how God gathers His children under His wings. What bird did I describe in this illustration? (Luke 13:34) (a) dove, (b) hen, (c) pigeon, (d) pelican, (e) none of the above.

11. I released pigeons as I tried to encourage proper focus on temple worship. Who am I? (John 2:16) (a) Abraham, (b) David, (c) Solomon, (d) Ezra, (e) Jesus.

12. My name is John and like one of the Old Testament prophets I saw a creature with the face of a bird. What bird was depicted? (Revelation 4:6-8) (a) Ostrich, (b) Pelican, (c) Eagle, (d) Robin.

ANSWERS: *(1) a-Noah, (2) b-Abraham, (3) d-Moses, (4) a-Elijah, (5) c-Angels (the word "angel" is never used with the word "wings"), (6) c-Ezekiel, (7) d-Jonah, (8) a-sparrow, (9) c-Mary and Joseph, (10) b-hen, (11) e-Jesus, (12) c-Eagle.*

SCORING: 12 correct—You score is great and it's not "for the birds", 11 or 10 correct—you are not a dumb cluck; 9 correct—you did not lay an egg with your answers; 8 or fewer correct—fly to the Bible for even more information.

Black Friday in the Bible

(The phrase "Black Friday" has come to describe the day after Thanksgiving when most retailers pull out all of the stops in trying to insure that they will go "in the black" (from red ink) for the Christmas holiday and the rest of the year. Some have even suggested that many retailers are "in the red" for most of the year and need a day like "Black Friday" with their Black Friday "specials" to change their fortunes for the year.)

1. Abraham's wife Sarah died and Abraham found himself in a strange land that God had promised would eventually be his. On this sad and Black Friday Abraham needed a burial plot for Sarah and he purchased from Hittites a graveyard for Sarah. What was the location of this land which was the only land in his lifetime that Abraham would own in the Promised Land? (Genesis 23:9) (a) the Cave of Machpelah, (b) a plot in Jerusalem, (c) land in Bethlehem, (d) the Temple Mount.

2. During a severe famine in Egypt it was a dark time and the Egyptian people ended up selling themselves and their property to their nation's ruler, the Pharaoh, in a Black Friday event. Who was in charge of this "sale"? (Genesis 49:18-20) (a) Jacob, (b) David, (c) Joseph, (d) Benjamin.

3. It wasn't Black Friday but When Solomon was building the Temple he negotiated with this builder so that the cedars of Lebanon could be used. Name this builder. (I Kings 5:6-8) (a) Saul of Tarsus, (b) Gideon, (c) Jephthan, (d) Hiram of Tyre.

4. When a severe famine unfolded in Samaria at the time of Elisha and Ben-hadad who was the king of Syria, the following Black Friday "sales" were part of dealing with this famine. What was being "sold" and consumed. (II Kings 6:24-29) (a) sale of donkey's heads for food, (b)

dung from doves, (c) boiled children for food, (d) all of the above, (e) none of the above.

5. Jesus told a Black Friday parable about a group of young women who were foolish and wise. It wasn't Black Friday but Jesus said that at any time a "farthing" or a "penny" could buy how many sparrows? (Matthew 10:29) (a) one, (b) two, (c) three, (d) seven.

6. The foolish young women didn't make proper preparations for the wedding that they were attending and they ended up going out on Black Friday to purchase more oil for their depleted lamps. How many of these young women were foolish? (Matthew 25:1-13) (a) one, (b) two, (c) three, (d) five, (e) ten.

7. The day on which Jesus died is sometimes called "Black Friday" but more often we call it Good Friday. The soldiers didn't purchase his clothing but what did they do to secure Jesus' garment? (Matthew 27:35) (a) tore it from Him, (b) they gambled for it, (c) received it as a gift from priests, (d) a man named Turin gave it to them.

8. This magician was so impressed with the work that Peter and John were doing, he wanted to purchase this power from them, perhaps in a Black Friday sale. Peter told him, "May your silver perish with you because you thought that you could obtain the gift of God with money." What was this man's name? (Acts 8:9-20) (a) Ananias, (b) Philip, (c) Simon, (d) Felix.

9. Paul also got into trouble with some people who owned a certain commodity. What did Paul do on this Black Friday to upset the people? (Acts 16:16-24) (a) healed a slave girl who could tell the future, (b) preached and healed in the Roman temple where they sold food, (c) got rid of the golden snakes, (d) destroyed idols in a market place stand.

10. When Paul was preaching in Ephesus he caused one of the merchants to be very upset with his work. This Black Friday led to a near riot which was quelled by the city

clerk. What was the concern of these merchants? (Acts 19:25-27) (a) Paul was stealing members from them, (b) their books weren't selling, (c) they could no longer sell their Artemis idols, (d) all of the above.

ANSWERS: (1) a/Cave of Machpelah; (2) c/Joseph; (3) d/Hiram of Tyre; (4) d/all of the above; (5) b/two; (6) d/five; (7) b/they gambled for it; (8) c/Simon; (9) a/healed a slave girl who could tell the future; (10) c/they could no longer sell their Artemis idols.

SCORING: 10 Correct: Your score is a real bargain; 9 Correct: You only missed one "special"!; 8 correct: Just keep on shopping for answers!; 7 correct: Don't fret, there will always be another "sale".

Bowls in the Bible

(Many "Bowl" games are played in December and January and one of the last major bowl games is the "Super Bowl." Does the Bible say anything about "bowls"? Not really…though the Bible talks about bowls (including dishes and vessels) as containers for food or other items. Why not consider this unusual quiz about "Bowls in the Bible" to test your skill with the pages of Scripture. If you need help, you may wish to check the Bible passage given. If the Bible reference would give away the answer only the verse is given.)

1. I wrote to Timothy about vessels of gold and silver as well as vessels of wood and earth. Some vessels honor and some dishonor. Who am I? (II Timothy 2:20) (a) Paul, (b) Titus, (c) Peter, (d) John.

2. At a supper with my followers I said that the one who dipped his hand with me in the dish would end up betraying me. (Matthew 26:23) Who am I? (a) Herod, (b) Judas, (c) Jesus, (d) Simon Peter.

3. My name is Solomon and I wrote about the "golden bowl" being broken (Ecclesiastes 12:6). What was I talking about? (a) Breaking a leg, (b) murder, (c) war, (d) death.

4. In my book (Jeremiah 52:18) I wrote about the shovels, snuffers, bowls, spoons, brass vessels and other things. What was I referring to? (a) items in the Temple being taken away in the Babylonian captivity, (b) how the Temple was decorated, (c) things that God did not allow in the Temple, (d) donations made to the Jews by Nebuchadnezzar.

5. In my book I wrote about people drinking wine in bowls and anointing themselves with ointment. What were the people not doing? (Amos 6:6) (a) not going to church, (b) not caring about the affliction of Joseph, (c) not tithing, (d) not singing.

6. I wasn't sure that I really believed that God was calling me to a certain task and wringing out water into a bowl was part of the "test." (Judges 6:38) Who am I? (a) Samson, (b) Jephthah, (c) Gideon, (d) Joshua.

7. I tricked my brother with a bowl of lentil stew. Who am I? (Genesis 25:29-34) (a) Abraham, (b) Isaac, (c) Esau, (d) Jacob, (e) Joseph.

8. When I wanted nothing to do with the execution of a righteous man, I washed my hands in a bowl of water. Who am I? (Matthew 27:24-25) (a) Herod, (b) Pontius Pilate, (c) Caesar Augustus, (d) Procurus.

9. On the night before I died on a cross I used a bowl to do the following (John 13:3-7): (a) wash the feet of my followers, (b) share the Passover, (c) distribute bread, (d) distribute figs.

10. My name is John and in Revelation chapter 16 I saw several bowls of wrath. How many bowls did I see? (a) three, (b) five, (c) seven, (d) nine.

11. It wasn't a bowl but it was a silver cup that I had placed in a sack of one of my relatives to make a point. Who am I? (Genesis 44:1-2) (a) Moses, (b) Joshua, (c) Joseph, (d) David, (e) Jeremiah.

12. I gave the leader of the enemy army a bowl of milk when he entered my tent and then assassinated him with a tent peg. (Judges 4:19-21, Judges 5:25). Who am I? (a) Deborah, (b) Barak, (c) Jael, (d) Delilah.

ANSWERS: *(1) a/Paul; (2) c/Jesus; (3) d/death; (4) a/items in the Temple being taken away in the Babylonian captivity; (5) b/not caring about the affliction of Joseph; (7) d/Jacob; (8) b/Pontius Pilate; (9) a/wash he feet of my followers; (10) c/seven; (11) c/Joseph; (12) c/Jael*

SCORING: If you got all 15 correct, you are ready to visit Bethlehem and see Jesus, the "bread of life." If you scored 13 or 14 correct you have the "ingredients" for a Christ-filled Christmas. If you scored 11 or 12 correct you realize the nuggets of truth that God reveals to us. If you scored 10 or fewer correct you need to be careful and check the "recipe" for bread that God reveals in to us in His Word.

Bread in the Bible

(Bread is one of the staples of life itself. During the Advent and Christmas season we hear a lot about the city of Bethlehem, the place where Jesus Christ was born. The meaning of the word "Bethlehem" is "House of Bread" and from this "house" we receive the "Bread of Life" which is what Jesus calls Himself in John 6:35. Take this little True/False quiz on "bread" and test to see if you are ready to greet Jesus in the "house of bread." If you need help, you may wish to check the Bible passage given.)

1. True/False. After his sin in the Garden of Eden God told Adam that he would eat bread "by the sweat" of his brow or face. (Genesis 3:19)

2. True/False. After Abram (later known as Abraham) rescued his nephew Lot the king of Salem named Melchizedek blessed him and brought him bread and wine while Abram responded with a tithe (Genesis 14:18-19).

3. True/False. God fed His people in the wilderness with "bread from heaven" which was also called "manna" or, literally, "What is it?" (Exodus 16:4).

4. True/False. The "Bread of Presence" in the Temple was actual bread that God's people were to keep on display in the Tabernacle and later the Temple. (Exodus 35:13)

5. True/False. God told His people that they should (and would) not live "by bread alone" but by God's Word (Deuteronomy 8:3).

6. True/False. The prophet Isaiah wrote that the rain and snow which God provides helps to give "seed to the Sower and bread to the eater" (Isaiah 55:10).

7. True/False. Jesus taught us to pray for our "daily bread" (Matthew 6:11, Luke 11:3).

8. True/False. The Bible records that Jesus fed at least 5000 people using five loaves of bread and two fish (Mark 6:38-44).

9. True/False. The Bible records that Jesus fed at least 4000 people using seven loaves of bread and a "few small fish" (Mark 8:5-9).

10. True/False. At the Passover meal with His disciples Jesus took bread and blessed it and said "Take, this is my body" (Mark 14:22).

11. True/False. After His death on the cross and His resurrection Jesus spent time with two disciples travelling to Emmaus and became known to them in the "breaking of the bread" (Luke 24:35).

12. True/False. Near the Sea of Galilee Jesus asked His disciple, Philip, where they were going to be able to "buy bread" to feed the large crowd which had gathered (John 6:5-6).

13. True/False. One of the four "signs" of the work of the church was the Lord's Supper or "the breaking of the bread" (Acts 2:42).

14. True/False. The people of the early church attended the Temple together, broke bread in their homes and received their food with "glad and generous hearts" (Acts 2:46).

15. True/False. In his letter to the Corinthians the Apostle Paul says that the "bread that we break" is a "participation" or "communion" in the body of Christ (I Corinthians 10:16).

ANSWERS: This could be a tricky quiz. All of the statements in this quiz are "True" according to the Bible passages noted.

SCORING: If you got all 15 correct, you are ready to visit Bethlehem and see Jesus, the "bread of life." If you scored 13 or 14 correct you have the "ingredients" for a Christ-filled Christmas. If you scored 11 or 12 correct you realize the nuggets of truth that God reveals to us. If you scored 10 or fewer correct you need to be careful and check the "recipe" for bread that God reveals in to us in His Word.

Callings in the Bible

(In the summer months when many churches say farewell to pastors who are retiring and those following other calls and callings. In addition, it is a time of year for people to consider vocations following the Lord's will and work. In the Bible quiz below, see if you can determine the name or information about the various people called by God to be prophets, priests and kings. If the reference gives away the answer, only the Scripture verse is noted.)

1. I was a great and mysterious priest who was called "king of Salem" and in the book of Hebrews was referred to as a priest forever. (Genesis 14:18) My name is (a) Samuel, (b) Abraham, (c) Melchizedek, (d) Moses.

2. In the pages of the Bible I am called a judge, a priest, and a prophet. Since I was an answer to prayer, my mother dedicated me to the Lord at a young age and had me live in the Temple and learn from an aging priest. (1:21-26) My name is (a) Moses, (b) Samuel, (c) Isaiah, (d) David.

3. My greatest objection to being called to God's service was my age—I said I was too young and only a child. (1:6-8). My name is (a) Moses (b) Samuel (c) Jeremiah, (d) Hannaiah.

4. I leaped in my mother's womb at the news of the birth of the Messiah. My relatives wanted to name me "Zechariah" but my mother gave me the name revealed to her by an angel. (Luke 1:39-45) My name was and is (a) John (b) Jesus (c) Joseph (d) Herod.

5. Though it took me many years to get where God wanted me to be, my whole life, from my rescue in a little ark to my childhood in Pharaoh's temple, to my shepherding days with my father-in-law was all under the guidance of God. (Exodus 2:1-10) My name is (a) Noah, (b) Japheth, (c) Abraham, (d) Moses.

6. My name is Abraham and my call was mostly to believe the promises of God as revealed in (Genesis 12-22) (a) a smoking firepot moving through a cut up animal, (b) an appearance of three "men" on their way to destroy a city, (c) an prayerful argument with a man about God's will about the wicked, (d) promise of a son to be born when I was 100 years old, (e) all of the above, (f) none of the above.

7. I was called on the Damascus road and in a blinding light was urged to stop hurting and harming the body of Christ. (Acts 9:1-9) My name is (a) Timothy, (b) Saul, (c) Titus, (d) Barnabas, (e) Silas.

8. The Bible says that my mother and my grandmother were both instrumental in leading me to serve as a pastor in the church. My name is (1:5) (a) Paul, (b) John the Baptist, (c) Timothy, (d) John the Apostle.

9. I told an unbelieving king that I was neither a prophet nor the son of a prophet, but a shepherd who was called by God to bring a message to God's people. (7:12-15) My name is (a) Amaziah, (b) Israel, (c) Jeremiah, (d) Amos, (e) none of the above.

10. My name is John, also known as the "disciple whom Jesus loved." One of the five following statements is not true about my life and my work as a servant of Jesus. (a) I had a brother named James. (b) I wrote five New Testament books. (c) I am called the "elder" in books that I wrote. (d) I was a fisherman. (e) I wrote the book of Acts.

11. My name is Isaiah and when I was called to serve I experienced (Isaiah 6:1-9) (a) being struck without speech for several months, (b) an angel of God putting a hot coal on my tongue, (c) being transported by my hair to Babylon to see God's people in exile, (d) the need to write to the 7 churches of Asia Minor, (e) a vision in a burning bush.

12. My name is Noah and as God's servant to rescue the world from a universal flood, I found myself called to the

task of (Genesis 6-7) (a) gathering seven pairs of clean animals, (b) rescuing 7 other human beings, (c) gathering a pair of unclean animals, (d) preaching a message of repentance, (e) all of the above, (f) none of the above.

ANSWERS*: (1) c, (2) b, (3) c, (4) a, (5) d, (6) e, (7) b, (8) c, (9) d, (10) e, (11) b, (12) e.*

SCORING: 12 Correct: You are ready to follow the Lord's leading; 11 Correct: You know where you are going!; 10 Correct: It is challenging to follow the Lord's will; 9 or fewer Correct: Just listen to the voice of the Lord as to where you will be sent.

Caregiving in the Old Testament

("Caregivers" are individuals or groups who help others with the daily activities of life and living. The term is being used more and more to describe paid or unpaid individuals who provide help of all sorts with disabilities, medical challenges, and times of convalescence or other short or long term needs. Are caregivers described in the Bible? Perhaps. See if you can determine the unique care giving situation being described in the Old Testament. Use the Bible clue if you need help. The Bible book is not mentioned in the clue if it would give away the answer.)

1. I told God that I was not a caregiver to my brother. In fact, I said, "Am I my brother's keeper?" What was my name? (Genesis 4:8-9) (a) Adam, (b) Cain, (c) Noah, (d) Seth, (e) Methuselah.

2. My name is Abraham and more than once I had to rescue and take care of my nephew. Once I had to separate from him and I offered him first choice of land on which to settle. Another time he was captured in a raid and a third time he found himself in peril in an evil city. Thank God I was able to be a caregiver for him in each case. Do you know his name? (Genesis 13:8-10, Genesis 14:16, Genesis 19) (a) Isaac, (b) Ishmael, (c) Lot, (d) Melchizedek

3. I rescued the first-born son of Abraham when he and his mother were banished by Abraham's jealous wife. They found themselves in grave danger in the desert but I rescued them and delivered a promise for the ages. Who am I? (Genesis 21:17-20) (a) Abimelech, (b) God Himself, (c) Ishmael, (d) Eliezer

4. More than once I had to serve as a caregiver to others. First it was to my father and brothers. Then it was to a man named Potiphar. Later I gave care to a baker and the king's cup bearer. Then I was caregiver to the king himself. And, finally, I again was caretaker for my brothers and

father. Do you know my name? (Genesis 37:5-8, Genesis 39:1-6, Genesis 40, Genesis 41:25-33, Genesis 41:39-40, Genesis 46:1-7) (a) David, (b) Elijah, (c) Abraham, (d) Joseph.

5. I was Pharaoh's daughter and I "found" a baby floating in a little boat on the water. I couldn't bear to see him perish so I took care of him by finding a caregiver for him who ended up being his very mother. What was this baby's name? (Exodus 2:5-10) (a) Aaron, (b) Ramses, (c) Moses, (d) Joshua.

6. I cared for our leader, Moses, and was his protégé and eventually his successor when he went up on Mount Nebo to die. I was the "son of Nun" and Moses "laid his hands" on me when I was named as his successor. What's my name? (Deuteronomy 34:9) (a) Caleb, (b) Joshua, (c) Korah, (d) Aaron

7. Our names aren't that important but our son became a famous judge in Israel. We were "caregivers" to him but it seemed that he often did not want to follow our advice. He was as strong as an ox but didn't always make the wisest of decisions. That's the perils of being a caregiver. What was our son's name? (Judges 13) (a) Uriah, (b) Gideon, (c) Samson, (d) Jonathan.

8. My name is David and I was Saul the King's son in law and also his successor. Some would suggest that I was instrumental in his downfall but you have to read the book and form your own opinion. Saul's son was my best friend and after his death I found myself serving as a caregiver to help for this crippled man. What was his name? (II Samuel 9) (a) Jonathan, (b) Mephibosheth, (c) Absalom, (d) Solomon.

9. When King David was old I was employed as a special helper to him in his infirm old age. People today might think that my role was at times astonishing, but this was my calling. What was my name? (I Kings 1:1-4) (a) Abishag, (b) Bathsheba, (c) Sheba, (d) Shunama

10. In some ways I was a caregiver to my mentor, Elijah. I was chosen to follow him as a prophet but he kept telling me to stay where I was but I wouldn't hear of it. I followed him until the time when he was taken up to heaven. Do you know my unique name? (II Kings 2:1, 11-12) (a) Gehazi, (b) Enoch, (c) Elisha, (d) Balak

11. I wasn't so much a caregiver as I was a parent. I raised my uncle's daughter and was a father and caregiver to a woman who attained great status in the kingdom of Persia after the king's wife was banished. In fact, she became the Queen. Her name was Esther but what was my name? (Esther 2:5-7) (a) Haman, (b) Mordecai, (c) Xerxes, (d) Jeremiah.

12. Most people would not think of me as being a caregiver, however, I served God by eventually caring for people in need. My first inclination, however, was to run away from God. However, God will not allow this to happen. I had to swallow my pride after God had me swallowed and I cared by preaching to people who could scarcely understand their right hand from their left hand. Technically, I was disappointed when they turned to the Lord. What's my name? (1:1, 3:6-9) (a) Hosea, (b) Joel, (c) Amos, (d) Jonah, (e) Obadiah

ANSWERS: (1) b-Cain, (2) c-Lot, (3) b-God Himself, (4) d-Joseph, (5) c-Moses, (6) b-Joshua, (7) c-Samson, (8) b-Mephibosheth, (9) a-Abishag, (10) c-Elisha, (11) b-Mordecai, (12) d-Jonah.

SCORING: 12 correct—You care and you give!; 11 or 10 correct—You care enough to know the Scripture; 9—You are always learning to care; 8 or fewer correct—It's never too late to learn to care!

"Christmas According to John's Gospel"

(The Gospels of Matthew and Luke in the New Testament give us unique details about the birth of Jesus. Matthew especially focuses on Joseph, King Herod and the Magi. Luke especially focuses on Mary, the angels, the birth in Bethlehem, the shepherds and the early life of Jesus. Mark's short Gospel doesn't contain any information on the birth of Jesus but John's Gospel approaches the birth of Jesus in a somewhat mystical and philosophical fashion, using the word "Word" (or "logos" in the Greek) to describe Jesus. In this quiz below, based on the first 18 verses of John 1 the Gospel writer is referring to Jesus even though His name is not used until verse 17. See how much you know about this unique but somewhat obscure version of the Christmas story.)

1. John writes that this was in the "beginning" and was "with God" and "was God." (John 1:1) He is referring to (a) the Spirit, (b) Santa Claus, (c) snow, (d) John, (e) Jesus.

2. According to John's Gospel (John 1:3-4) (a) through Jesus all things were made, (b) without Jesus nothing was made, (c) Jesus was the light and life of men, (d) all of the above.

3. John contrasts light and darkness and says that (John 1:5) (a) the light doesn't understand, (b) the darkness doesn't understand, (c) John doesn't understand, (d) Jesus doesn't understand.

4. The opening verses of John tell that this man was a witness to the light (John 1:6-8): (a) Jesus, (b) John, (c) Peter, (d) Andrew.

5. In John's Christmas story the world (John 1:10) (a) celebrates Christmas with manger scenes, (b) celebrates Christmas with angels and shepherds, (c) does not recognize Jesus, (d) celebrates the birth of John rather than the birth of Jesus.

6. The opening words of the Gospel of John say that all who believe in His name (John 1:12) (a) are members of the

church, (b) are children of God, (c) are disciples, (d) are part of the invisible church.

7. When writing about the glory of God in Jesus the writer John says (John 1:14) (a) they saw his glory, (b) that no one saw his glory, (c) that everyone in the world saw His glory, (e) that only the disciples saw His glory, (e) that there is no glory.

8. John says that the "Word" (John 1:14) (a) is contained only in the pages of the Bible, (b) became flesh and dwelt among us, (c) is a unique idea referring to God the Holy Spirit, (d) was a human invention.

9. According to John 1:14 Jesus or the "Word" is (a) invisible to everyone, (b) only a figment of people's imagination, (c) full of grace and truth, (d) none of the above.

10. John described Jesus as one (John 1:15) (a) who comes after me, (b) who surpassed him, (c) who was before him, (d) all of the above, (e) none of the above.

11. In a deep theological statement John says that because of the fullness of His grace (John 1:16) (a) we receive one blessing after another, (b) we are going to heaven, (c) we are able to do good works, (d) we are children of Abraham.

12. John says that (John 1:18) (a) God is visible to all who believe, (b) God is Triune, (c) God is invisible to all people, (d) no one has ever seen God.

ANSWERS: 1 (e), 2 (d), 3 (b), 4 (b), 5 (c), 6 (b), 7 (a), 8 (b), 9 (c), 10 (d), 11 (a), 12 (d).

SCORING: 12 or 11 correct (You are into the Word), 10 correct (You are ready for Christmas), 9 or 8 correct (You need to reread John's Gospel account), 7 or fewer correct (Turn on the light!).

Cities in the Bible

(Shortly after the creation of the world, people began to group themselves together in cities. In the New Year we may find ourselves visiting many different cities for many different reasons. Supply, if you can, the names of the Biblical cities described in these questions.)

1. The walls of this city, often regarded as one of the oldest in the world, got very "shook" when God's people played a loud tune. *(Joshua 6:20)*

2. This city was really a "crying shame" as Jesus wept over it. *(Matthew 23:37)*

3. The blueprints for this city got slightly confused when God got angry with the workmen's defiance. *(Genesis 11:8-9)*

4. Nathaniel wondered if anything good could come from this city. Eventually, he found out. *(John 1:46)*

5. This city wasn't built in a day and it took Paul a lot longer to get there. *(Acts 23:11)*

6. This city wasn't known for very much, except that it was the birthplace of the two greatest kings of the Bible. *(Matthew 2:6)*

7. There was a "hot time" in these towns when God's righteous anger was kindled against them. *(Genesis 19:24)*

8. Jonah fled from this city; in the New Testament Paul claimed this same city as his home. *(Jonah 1:3)*

9. The first murderer, Cain, named this city after his son. *(Genesis 4:17-18)*

10. Every sin under the sun could be found in this city and Paul had to write several letters to the Christian people there. *(Acts 18:1)*

11. This city captured the imagination of God's people as well as their bodies for a period of captivity. *(Psalm 137:1)*

12. The Christians in this city were like boy scouts--well prepared. In fact, they were so ready for Christ's second coming that they neglected their normal duties. *(II Thessalonians 3:11-13)*

13. These Christians were like people from the "Show Me" state of Missouri. They checked the Scriptures carefully to verify what was being preached. *(Acts 17:11)*

14. This city of brotherly love in Asia was complimented in the book of Revelation for its faithfulness. *(Revelation 3:7ff.)*

15. These cities were places in the Old Testament where people "on the run" could stay. *(Numbers 35:11)*

*(**ANSWERS**: 1-Jericho, 2-Jerusalem, 3-Babel, 4-Nazareth, 5-Rome, 6-Bethlehem, 7-Sodom/Gomorrah, 8-Tarshish, 9-Enoch, 10-Corinth, 11-Babylon, 12-Thessalonica, 13-Berea, 14-Philadelphia, 15-Refuge)*

SCORING – 15 or 14 correct – You know your cities!; 12 or 13 correct – You know how to get places; 10 or 11 correct – Check your maps for more information; less than 10 correct – Are you lost?

Clergy Appreciation in the Bible

(October is Clergy Appreciation month. We do honor and appreciate all who have brought the Word of God into our lives. They are God's human instruments to bring us to faith in Jesus and to guide us in our spiritual lives. Individuals in the Bible sometimes felt appreciated and sometimes did not. See if you can determine the person being described in these questions and statements about clergy, pastors, ministers, and other church leaders.)

1. I was priest of a mysterious place called Salem and I had the sacred responsibility of ministering to Abraham and others. He presented tithes and offerings to the Lord as I ministered to him. My name is unusual but the author of the book of Hebrews spends a great deal of time talking about me and my work as a priest. (Genesis 14:18-20, Hebrews 7) My name is (a) Ezekiel, (b) Amminidab, (c) Melchizedek, (d) Oz.

2. My name is Samuel and my priest and mentor was a great leader of God's people who failed to minister properly to the Lord as his life continued. His ministry to my mother, however, was exactly what God wanted him to do. His ministry to me when God called me in the night was also on target. What was the name of this special priest and minister? (I Samuel 3:1-18) (a) Moses, (b) Aaron, (c) Eli, (d) Nathan.

3. Talk about a difficult job! I was priest to the king and I had to tell him about terrible sins which he had committed. No one who ministers for the Lord enjoys doing such a thing, but that was my calling. (II Samuel 12:1-7) What was my name? (a) Nathan, (b) Aaron, (c) Job, (d) Haggai.

4. During the time of King Josiah the priest came to me, a female prophetess, to inquire about the discovery of the book of the law. Though I brought difficult news to the king about what would happen to God's people I assured

him that he would not see the disaster which was to come. (II Kings 22:14) What was my name? (a) Hilkiah, (b) Shallum, (c) Huldah, (d) Jezebel.

5. My husband and I helped to ensure that a young eloquent pastor who was a protégé of the Apostle Paul would know how to better speak the Word of God. (Acts 18:24-26) What was my name? (a) Mary Magdalene, (b) Dorcas, (c) Joanna, (d) Priscilla.

6. The Apostle John, our trusted minister, addressed me in a special way in his second epistle. He recognized how important I was to the church. (II John 1) He referred to me as (a) the chosen lady, (b) the queen of heaven, (c) the queen of the south, (d) chosen sister.

7. Though my brother was much more famous than I was and was the leader of God's people out of Egypt, I became his spokesman and served as minister and priest to the people. (Exodus 4:14-16) My name was (a) Joshua, (b) Jochebed, (c) Lot, (d) Aaron.

8. My name is Amos and when I was chosen to serve God's people, all of the following were true except, (Amos 1:14) (a) I was not a prophet, (b) I was not a prophet's son, (c) I was a shepherd, (d) I took care of sycamore fig trees, (e) all of the above are true.

9. I appreciated the work of my prophet and minister. Through the Lord God he provided for me and my son with a cruise of oil that did not fail. His name was (I Kings 17:7-16) (a) Nain, (b) Elisha, (c) Elijah, (d) Eliphaz, (e) Ezekiel.

10. Jesus ministered to me and to my brother and my sister. It is said that while my sister was bothered by "busy work," like a disciple, I sat at his feet and listened and learned. (Luke 10:38-42) What is my name? (a) Martha, (b) Miriam, (c) Marsha, (d) Mary, (e) none of the above.

11. I dedicated my long-awaited son to the Lord. My husband had another wife named Peninnah and she made fun of me. My husband was loving and patient with me but I

still wanted a son and when he was born I was so thankful that I declared that he would "minister" before the Lord. (I Samuel 1:8-11) What was my name? (a) Elkanah, (b) Hannah, (c) Haggai, (d) Nazir

12. Though my husband was the one who ministered to the Lord, God made a promise to him and to me that resulted in one of the greatest ministers and servants of all. He refused to be acknowledged as a prophet, but this is precisely what he was. My husband had been struck speechless by the news but, when asked, wrote his name of our "minister" son for all to see. (Luke 1:13) What is my name? (a) Mary, (b) Zacharias, (c) Herodias, (d) Elizabeth.

13. My life of fasting and prayer led to my encounter with the baby Jesus. I was a prophetess and after holding Jesus I gave thanks to God and spoke about Him to many people. (Luke 1:36-38). What is my name? (a) Anna, (b) Phanuel, (c) Elizabeth, (d) Rachel.

ANSWERS: *(1) c, (2) c, (3) a, (4) c, (5) d, (6) a, (7) d, (8) e, (9) c, (10) d, (11) b, (12) d, (13) a*

SCORING: 13 Correct: We appreciate your perfect score; 12 Correct: You appreciate those who are clergy; 11 Correct: It's a joy to serve; 10 or fewer to Correct: The more the learn, the more you appreciate!

Communication in the Bible

(We have many forms of communication in our world today with the "Internet" and E-mail and Social Media being some of the newest forms. We add to this cell phones, pagers, and a host of other ways of getting in touch and staying in touch with people in our lives. God has always stayed in touch with us through His unique forms of communication. See if you can determine the person with whom God communicated from the clues given.)

1. God communicated with me through a burning bush. Who am I? *(Exodus 3:1-6)*
2. God communicated with me by causing my striped cattle to multiply faster and thus prospered me. Who am I? *(Genesis 30:31-43)*
3. I was sad when God communicated with me and said that I could not build His temple. Who am I? *(I Chronicles 28:2-3)*
4. I was told to write 7 letters to 7 churches and thus communicate with them. Who am I. *(Revelation 1:1-5)*
5. A big fish swallowed me. Talk about an unusual communiqué. Who am I? *(Jonah 1:17)*
6. Facing down evil prophets on Mt. Carmel was a tough way of communicating but God sent a great fire to consume my offering. In this way He spoke to me and the people. Who am I? *(I Kings 18:16-39)*
7. God's rainbow in the clouds communicated to me and the world that there would never be another worldwide flood. Who am I? *(Genesis 9:12-16)*
8. A terrible lesson was communicated to me and to God's people when I accidentally touched His sacred ark. Who am I? *(I Chronicles 13:9-10)*

9. I was called the "word made flesh" in John's Gospel and I was God's ultimate way of communicating. Who am I? *(John 1:1-3, 14)*

10. Three men visited me and later visited the evil cities of Sodom and Gomorrah. Who am I? *(Genesis 18)*

11. My offering of grain was communicated to God with an insincere heart. Who am I? *(Genesis 4:3-5)*

12. In Caesarea God communicated with me in a dream by lowering a tablecloth full of food to me. Though I felt that some of the food was unclean, God made His point. Who am I? *(Acts 10:9-16)*

13. I saw a "ladder" or stairway to heaven. What a wonderful way God communicated with me! Who am I? *(Genesis 28:10-12)*

14. God blinded me on the Damascus Road. Talk about getting my attention. Who am I? *(Acts 9:1-6)*

15. I was brought back from the dead by Peter so that I could continue to sew items for the poor. Who am I? *(Acts 9:36)*

16. In the pain of childbirth God communicated with me in the Garden of Eden and told me my progeny would include a Savior for mankind. Who am I? *(Genesis 3:15-16)*

ANSWERS: *(1) Moses, (2) Jacob, (3) David, (4) John, (5) Jonah, (6) Elijah, (7) Noah, (8) Uzzah, (9) Jesus, (10) Abraham, (11) Cain, (12) Peter, (13) Jacob, (14) Paul, (15) Dorcas, (16) Eve*

SCORING: 15 or 14 correct: You are speaking and listening well; 13 or 12 correct: "Speak, Lord, your servant is listening"; Less than 12 correct: Is there a communication problem?

Dancing in the Bible

(People have differing opinions about dancing, but there were many times in the Bible when people danced. Several decades ago a song about Jesus titled "Lord of the Dance" (arranged by Sydney Carter) suggested that the life of Jesus expressed a joyful attitude as he "danced" through life and effected our salvation. One of the verses reads, with Jesus as the singer:

But I am the dance and I still go on.
Dance then, wherever you may be
I am the Lord of the Dance said he
And I'll lead you all wherever you may be,
And I'll lead you all in the Dance said he.

More recently, a song performed by Lee Ann Womack said, "I Hope You Dance." It referred to how we react to situations. The song suggests:

When you come close to sellin' out, reconsider,
Give the heavens above more than just a passing glance,
And when you get the choice to sit it out or dance.
I hope you dance...I hope you dance.

(Some may not see this song as being spiritual but many Christian people appreciate the spiritual depth of these lyrics. In any case, see if you can determine the individual or nation being sought in the Biblical situations below (both good and bad) which speak about dancing. Check the Biblical reference if you need more help.)

1. This troubled tribe was censured by the other tribes of Israel and was told to see wives among the daughters of Shiloh "when they come out to dance." Which tribe is this? (Judges 21:20-21).
2. This famous king and ancestor of the Messiah, Jesus Christ, "danced" before the Lord. (II Samuel 6:14)

3. This man wrote of "a time to mourn and a time to dance." (Ecclesiastes 3:4).
4. In warning of judgment, God says that this great nation will become desolate and "satyrs shall dance there" (Isaiah 13:19-21)
5. This woman danced before her father in law and desired, at the insistence of her mother, an unusual reward of a human head. (Matthew 14:6)
6. This man rejected hypocrisy by charging that the people said of him, "We have piped unto you and you have not danced." (Matthew 11:7, 17)
7. When he saw dancing before an idol, this man became very angry (Exodus 32:19).
8. This king was met with music and dancing but he was upstaged by a more famous hero. Because of this he began to plot the death of this hero who later became his successor. (I Samuel 18:6-7).
9. In this parable the "Elder Brother" didn't like the music and dancing that honored his penniless younger brother who had returned and who was received by his father. (Luke 15:25)
10. This woman despised the fact that her husband danced before the Lord and she was punished accordingly (II Samuel 6:16).

ANSWERS: *(1) Benjamin, (2) David, (3) Solomon, (4) Babylon, (5) Herodias, (6) Jesus, (7) Moses, (8) Saul, (9) Prodigal Son, (10) Michal*

SCORING: 10 Correct: Dance for joy! 9 Correct: You know the right steps. 8 Correct: Keep practicing. 7 or fewer Correct: Learn a step at a time!

Dogs in the Bible

(More and more in society people are enjoying the "company" of pets and especially dogs to help them through difficult times. Dogs often give comfort. The Bible has some things to say about dogs and comfort. See if you can guess the incidents about dogs being described by using the clue which is given or by checking the Bible reference. If the name of the book would give the answer away the book is not named.)

1. Dogs are mentioned in the Bible (a) 10 times (b) 41 times (c) 105 times (d) more than 500 times.
2. In the Bible and in middle Eastern culture, except for Egypt, dogs were usually (a) wild scavengers (b) pets (c) worshiped as gods (d) none of the above
3. As God's people were ready to leave Egypt with the plague of the death of the firstborn God said the following would not happen (Exodus 11:7) (a) dogs would not bark at them, (b) dogs would go with them across the Red Sea, (c) dogs would become sacred idols in the wilderness, (d) dogs would no longer be eaten.
4. In the time of the Judges the individuals chosen to help Gideon defeat the Midianites were the ones who (Judges 7:5) (a) owned dogs to help with the attack (b) ate dogs (c) lapped water like a dog (d) none of the above.
5. This man said that David was treating him like a dog (I Samuel 17:43). What was his name? (a) Saul, (b) Shimei, (c) Samuel, (d) Goliath, (e) none of the above.
6. Even though this king was cursed like a dog by Shimei, he still protected this man and didn't allow his soldiers to put him to death (II Samuel 16:9-11): (a) King David (b) King Solomon (c) King Ahab (d) King Herod.
7. This Biblical king and queen literally "went to the dogs" at the time of their deaths (I Kings 21:24, 22:38): (a)

Ananias and Sapphira (b) Hosea and Gomer (c) Ahab and Jezebel (d) David and Bathsheba

8. This prophet's servant was referred to as "a mere dog" by Hazael but his prophecy was proved to be true (II Kings 8:13): (a) Elisha (b) Moses (c) Joel (d) Amos.

9. Sheep are mentioned repeatedly in the Bible but this is the only Bible book mentioning "sheep dogs" (30:1): (a) Exodus (b) Proverbs (c) Job (d) Psalms.

10. In the Messianic psalm, Psalm 22, which Jesus quoted from the cross the author cries out (Psalm 22:16, 20): (a) "Dogs have surrounded me" (b) "Deliver my precious life from the dogs" (c) neither "a" or "b" (d) Both "a" and b"

11. The writer of the book of Proverbs says just as a fool repeats his folly a dog does this (Proverbs 26:11): (a) attacks innocent beasts, (b) returns to its vomit, (c) keep barking at nothing, (d) lick people's sores.

12. In the book of Ecclesiastes the writer says that a live dog is better than this: (Ecclesiastes 9:4) (a) a dead lion, (b) a snake in the grass, (c) a friend in need, (d) food on the table.

13. In his Sermon on the Mount Jesus talks about various animals and says, "Do not give dogs" what is (Matthew 7:6) (a) meaty (b) reserved for humans (c) sacred or holy (d) the time of day.

14. The bold Canaanite woman in Matthew who sought Jesus' help for her daughter argued with Jesus about dogs and said (Matthew 15:26-27) (a) they should be killed (b) even the dogs eat crumbs from under the table (c) He shouldn't treat her daughter like a dog (d) dogs are man's best friend.

15. In the story of Lazarus and the Rich Man that Jesus told the dogs came to Lazarus and (Luke 16:21) (a) licked his sores (b) ate his bones (c) became his friends (d) dragged him away.

16. This prophetic book compares those outside the kingdom with wild dogs (22:15): (a) Isaiah (b) Jeremiah (c) Zechariah (d) Revelation.

ANSWERS: *(1) b-41times, (2) a-wild scavengers, (3) a-dogs would not bark at them, (4) c-lapped water like a dog, (5) d-Goliath, (6) a-King David, (7) c-Ahab and Jezebel, (8) a-Elisha, (9) c-Job, (10) d-both "a" and "b", (11) b-returns to his vomit, (12) a-a dead lion, (13) c-sacred or holy, (14) b-even the dogs eat crumbs from under the table, (15) a-licked his sores, (16) d-Revelation.*

SCORING: 16 correct—You are definitely "barking" up the right tree. 15 or 14 correct—Dogs can be your best friends, 13 or 12 correct—in this quiz the barking answers bite a little; 11 correct—No purebred dogs in the Bible; just check more on His pure Word! 10 correct or fewer—It's a "dog eat dog" world sometimes. Study up for a better score.

Disciples--Who's Who In the List of Disciples?

(Facebook talks about friends. Some have dozens and dozens of friends. Jesus was friendly with everyone but had 12 special friends who were His disciples ("disciplined followers") or apostles ("ones who were sent"). Match the short clue with the disciple names which are listed first in alphabetical order. If you need help, check the Biblical reference.)

Andrew - James – James the Less – John – Judas Iscariot – Judas Thaddeus - Matthew – Nathaniel - Philip - Simon Peter – Simon the Zealot – Thomas

1. _____ The new name Jesus gave me suggested I was a "rock." Who am I? (John 1:42)
2. _____ I asked Jesus, "We don't know where you are going; how can we know the way?" Who am I? (John 14:5)
3. _____ My name has Greek origins and I talked to Andrew and together he and I brought some Greek people to see Jesus. Who am I? (John 12:20-22)
4. _____ I was the first disciple to suffer death (martyrdom) after Jesus' death and resurrection. Who am I? (Acts 12:2)
5. _____ I was always listed last in every list of disciples and I held the moneybag for the group. Who am I? (Matthew 10:4, John 13:29)
6. _____ Matthew says that my name was "Bartholomew" but John records that I was the one who sarcastically asked about Jesus, "Can anything good come out of Nazareth?" Who am I? (John 1:46)
7. _____ I was a tax collector whose name was Levi but Jesus gave me a new name which suggests that I was "one who is sent." Who am I? (Matthew 9:9, Mark 2:13-14)

8. _____ Like Matthew, my father's name was Alphaeus but I had the same name as another disciple but apparently I was younger. Who am I? (Matthew 10:3, Mark 3:18)

9. _____ Almost nothing is known about me except for the fact that I shared a name with another disciple and may have been part of a radical group in Jerusalem. Who am I? (Luke 6:15)

10. _____ I brought a boy to Jesus who had 5 loaves of bread and 2 fish which Jesus used to feed more than 5000 people. Who am I? (John 6:8)

11. _____ I referred to myself as the "disciple whom Jesus loved" but Jesus also called me a "Son of Thunder". Who am I? (Mark 3:17, John 20:2)

12. _____ Matthew and Mark call me one name while Luke calls me "the son of James." Who am I? (Matthew 10:3, Luke 6:16)

ANSWERS: *(1) Simon Peter, (2) Thomas, (3) Philip, (4) James (5) Judas Iscariot (6) Nathaniel (7) Matthew, (8) James the Less, (9) Simon the Zealot (10) Andrew, (11) John, (12) Judas Thaddeus*

SCORING: 12 correct – You are friends with all of the disciples, even Judas; 10-11 – You know your disciple friends very well; 9 or fewer correct – God knows our name even when we do not know every name!

Exercise in the Bible

(With each New Year many people think about health matters and exercise. The Bible contains a few challenging references about "exercise." See if you can determine the answers in this "Exercise in the Bible Quiz." If you need help, check the Biblical reference. If the Bible reference would give away the answer, the Bible book is not given.)

1. Walking is good exercise and even though the Bible doesn't talk about my physical exercise it does say that I "walked" with God. Who am I? (Genesis 5:21) (a) Adam, (b) Eve, (c) Abel, (d) Enoch, (e) all of the above

2. I wrestled with God and it was a stalemate until God touched the nerve in my thigh and caused me to limp the rest of my life. Talk about nerve! Who am I? (Genesis 32:22-30) (a) Abraham, (b) Isaac, (c) Jacob, (d) Joseph

3. I was asked to climb up into the mountains to die. It wasn't the first time I climbed a mountain but at the end of my work, it was the last. Who Am I? *(*Deuteronomy 34:1-8*)* (a) Moses, (b) Abraham, (c) Isaac, (d) Jacob

4. I was a tremendous physical specimen with great power and was able to participate in great feats of strength until I lost my hair, my integrity and my freedom. Who am I? (Judges 16:18-21) (a) Elijah, (b) Elisha, (c) Samson, (d) Jonah

5. My exercise was working in the fields and gleaning wheat. My future husband allowed me to glean near the sheaves of grain. Who am I? (Ruth 2:8, 15-16) (a) Naomi, (b) Orpah, (c) Chilion, (d) Ruth

6. I ran to tell news of a battle to King David. I wasn't the person designated for the task but I outran the real messenger. Who am I? (II Samuel 18:19-33) (a) Jonathan, (b) Ahimaaz, (c) Absalom, (d) Solomon

7. Swimming is good exercise but I was a reluctant swimmer when I was thrown overboard and ended up being swallowed by a great fish. Who am I? (1:15-17) (a) Paul, (b) Noah, (c) Jonah, (d) Elijah

8. I ran away naked from the arrest of Jesus in the Garden of Gethsemane when Jesus was arrested. I am not named but my running is only recorded in one of the four gospels and that truth suggests that I was that man who ran away naked. Which Gospel writer am I? (14:51) (a) Matthew, (b) Mark, (c) Luke, (d) John

9. I was no athlete but I did kick in the womb when my mother and I met the young woman destined to be the mother of the Messiah, Jesus Christ. Who am I? (Luke 1:41, 63) (a) Mark (b) Simon Peter, (c) John the Baptist, (d) Jesus, (e) None of the above

10. In my ministry I talked a lot about "Olympic" events, include boxing and similar exercise. I even urged one of my successors to "fight the good fight of faith." Who am I? (I Timothy 6:12) (a) Paul, (b) Timothy, (c) Titus, (d) Stephen

ANSWERS: *1-(d) Enoch; 2-(c) Jacob; 3-(a) Moses; 4-(c) Samson, 5-(d) Ruth, 6-(b) Ahimaaz, 7-(c) Jonah, 8-(b) Mark, 9-(c) John the Baptist, 10-(a) Paul.*

SCORING: If you had 10 correct you have exercised your brain well. If you had 9 correct, you are almost perfect. If you had 8 or fewer correct you need to "get off the couch"!

Fall/Autumn in the Bible

(Fall is sometimes it is known as "autumn." The Bible speaks about seasons and about some of the things associated with this time of the year. See if you can determine the answers to this little quiz without checking the Biblical reference. If the book reference would give away the answer the book is not given.)

1. After this "event" in the Bible God said that seedtime and harvest and summer and winter and the seasons would not cease. What was this "event"? (Genesis 8:22) (a) the Fall of Adam and Eve, (b) Cain killing Abel, (c) the Flood, (d) the Tower of Babel.

2. This special festival (Numbers 29:1) was to be celebrated each year on the first day of the month in early autumn. What was this festival called? (a) Booths, (b) Trumpets, (c) Tabernacles, (d) all of the above.

3. Moses says that the following virtue will ensure that God will "give" autumn and spring rains (Deuteronomy 11:13-14) (a) piety, (b) obedience, (c) giving, (d) chastity.

4. This sad man, cupbearer to the king, found himself in late autumn of the year very sad about the plight of his people and his home area. The king, however, allowed him to go to Jerusalem to rebuild the walls of Jerusalem. Who was this sad man? (1:1, 1:11, 2:6) (a) Eli, (b) Samuel, (c) Ezra, (d) Nehemiah, (e) none of the above.

5. This place was called the "valley of tears" which referred to sorrow and sadness. Psalm 84:6 suggests that the spring or autumn rains would turn this area into a fertile place. What is this valley? (a) Baca, (b) Hinnom, (c) Sheol, (d) Zion, (e) none of the above.

6. The book of Proverbs (20:4) warns that this person does not plow in the fall and will thus not "find" a harvest in

his fields. What is this person called? (a) a sluggard, (b) a jackal, (c) an idolater, (d) a grasshopper.

7. Jeremiah speaks words of prophecy to people in this area who do not acknowledge God as God and as the provider of all blessings including autumn rain. To whom is Jeremiah writing and speaking (Jeremiah 5:24)? (a) Judah, (b) Jerusalem, (c) House of Jacob, (d) House of Israel, (e) all of the above.

8. This prophet who is sometimes known as the "grasshopper prophet" compares the autumn rains with the "rains" of God's righteousness on His people. Who was this prophet who wrote in verse 2:23? (a) Hosea, (b) Joel, (c) Amos, (d) Obadiah, (e) none of the above.

9. In some of his parting words this man said that it is not for us to know the times or seasons. Who was this leader (Acts 1:6)? (a) Peter, (b) Paul, (c) James, (d) Jesus.

10. This New Testament writer does not mention "fall" or "autumn" but he writes that he very concerning about some of the early Christians spending too much time in observing "days and months and seasons and years." Who was this writer (Galatians 4:10)? (a) Matthew, (b) Peter, (c) Paul, (d) James.

11. James, who is referred to as the "brother of the Lord" speaks about the patience of the farmer in waiting for the spring and fall rains. He compares this patience with the following Biblical character (James 5:7-11) (a) Abraham, (b) Jacob, (c) Daniel, (d) Job, (e) none of the above.

12. In a stinging rebuke of false religion the apostle Jude talks about fruitless trees in the fall of the year and mentions the following Biblical character who is a warning to us (Jude 1:11-12) (a) Cain, (b) Balaam, (c) Korah, (d) all of the above.

ANSWERS: *(1) c/the Flood; (2) d/all of the above, (3) b/obedience; (4) d/ Nehemiah; (5) a/Baca; (6) a/a sluggard; (7) e/all of the above; (8) b/Joel; (9) d/Jesus; (10) c/Paul; (11) d/Job; (12) d/all of the above.*

SCORING: 12 correct – You know what season this is and its meaning; 10-11 correct – You are springing forward with your careful analysis of weather patterns, 8-9 correct – You have caught the meaning of the seasons; 7 or fewer - bundle up for a more careful study of Scripture.

Fathers in the Bible

(Happy Father's Day on the third Sunday of June. Moms, Dads, and children would do well to consider the clues below and the father from the Bible being described. If you need help, check the Bible reference).

1. I was named "Father" of many nations. Who am I? *(Genesis 17:4-5)*
2. When I prayed in Gethsemane to my father I prayed, "Abba, Father." Who am I? *(Mark 14:36)*
3. I was spiritual father to a young pastor by the name of Timothy. Who am I? *(II Timothy 1:2)*
4. Jesus was my "son" and I was his earthly "adoptive" father. Who am I? *(Luke 3:23)*
5. When I learned that I would become the father of John the Baptist I was speechless! Who am I? *(Luke 1:12-13, 21-22)*
6. I was the father of Solomon, the great man of "peace." Who am I? *(I Kings 1:28-30)*
7. Fathering 12 sons who became the 12 tribes of Israel, I was happy that God blessed me. Who am I? *(Exodus 1:1-5)*
8. My twin sons did not always get along and the younger one ended up ruling over the older one. Who am I? *(Genesis 25:21-26)*
9. I was chagrined to father the first murderer in human history. Who am I? *(Genesis 4:1-10)*
10. I fathered 8 sons, one of whom was the greatest king of Israel and Judah. Who am I? *(I Samuel 16:10-13)*
11. By God's direction I married a harlot and fathered children. Who am I? *(Hosea 1:2-3)*
12. My three "rescued" sons were named Shem, Ham, and Japheth. Who am I? *(Genesis 10:1)*

13. I unknowingly fathered two nations through my sons and these nations became stumbling blocks for Israel. Who am I? *(Genesis 19:30-38)*
14. Fathering two sons in Egypt and rescuing my father and 11 brothers meant that my two sons would receive full shares in the Promised Land. Who am I? *(Genesis 48:17-20, Deuteronomy 33:16-17)*
15. I was the spiritual father of the prophet Elisha and I went to heaven in a fiery chariot. Who am I? *(II Kings 2:11-12)*

ANSWERS: (1) Abraham; (2) Jesus, (3) Paul, (4) Joseph, (5) Zechariah, (6) David, (7) Jacob, (8) Isaac, (9) Adam, (10) Jesse, (11) Hosea, (12) Noah, (13) Lot, (14) Joseph, (15) Elijah

SCORING: 14 or 15 correct--You know your fathers; 13 or 12 correct—You have paternal favor; 11 or fewer correct—Check with Dad for more help.

Fish in the Bible

(The 40 days of Lent have a tradition of fasting and especially fasting from meat on Fridays. Thus the alternative of fish is often suggested. Fish and fishing played a vital role in the life and ministry of Jesus and throughout the pages of the Bible. See if you can tell the fish or fishing event being described in this "Lenten" quiz, using the clue which is given or by checking the Bible reference.)

1. I declared that human beings would "rule over the fish of the sea" (Genesis 1:26, 28). Who am I? (a) God, (b) Abraham, (c) Moses, (d) Jesus, (e) none of the above.

2. I was told by God that "fear" and "dread" of me and all humans would be upon all earthly beasts, including the fish of the sea. (Genesis 9:2) Who am I? (a) Jonah, (b) Abraham, (c) Noah, (d) Satan, (e) none of the above.

3. My name is Moses and I obeyed God in "supervising" the Ten Plagues upon Egypt in order that my people would be free. The plague which caused the fish to die (Exodus 7:18-21) was the plague of (a) the death of the livestock, (b) the water becoming blood, (c) the flies, (d) the frogs, (e) none of the above.

4. We remembered the fish that we ate while in captivity in Egypt (Numbers 11:5) and angered God because of our complaining. We were the (a) Israelites, (b) Egyptians, (c) Canaanites, (d) Nazarenes, (e) none of the above.

5. I had great wealth and wisdom and the Bible says that I spoke 3000 proverbs and wrote 1005 songs, including many about animals and fish (I Kings 4:32-33). Who am I? (a) Saul, (b) David, (c) Solomon, (d) Job, (e) none of the above.

6. We were God's people and came back to Jerusalem to build many things including the "Sheep Gate" and the "Fish Gate." Where was the "Fish Gate" built? (Nehemiah

3:3) (a) Tabernacle, (b) main Temple, (c) the Synagogue, (d) the wall around the Temple.

7. I was part of the dialogue between Job and his so-called "friends" and I suggested that the "fish" should talk to them (Job 12:8). Who am I? (a) Job, (b) God, (c) Elihu, (d) Bildad, (e) Zophar.

8. My name is Jonah and I got into trouble with God. What does the Bible say "swallowed" me? (Jonah 1:17) (a) Brontosaurus, (b) Great Fish, (c) Whale, (d) Leviathan, (e) none of the above.

9. My name is Jesus and in my preaching I asked the question of when your son asks you for a fish would you give him (Matthew 7:10) (a) a piece of bread, (b) a rotten egg, (c) a snake (d) shrimp.

10. I am Andrew and when Jesus asked how a large crowd of 5000 men would be able to be fed I brought to him five loaves of bread and (Matthew 14:17) (a) one fish, (b) two fish, (c) three fish, (d) the Bible doesn't say how many.

11. When I saw a great draft of fish that Jesus helped us catch I fell on my knees and told him to go away from me because I was a sinful man. (Luke 5:4-8) Who am I? (a) Andrew, (b) John, (c) James, (d) Simon Peter, (e) all of the above

12. I am Simon Peter and Jesus taught me an important lesson about taxes and money when (Matthew 17:24-27) (a) He had me sell fish to get money, (b) He had Judas take money from the treasury to pay our tax, (c) He had me go fishing and I found a coin in the fish's mouth, (d) none of the above.

13. My name is Jesus and after the resurrection when I was hungry my disciples gave me (Luke 24:42) (a) two pickled fish, (b) a piece of broiled fish, (c) a piece of bread shaped like a fish, (d) none of the above.

14. My name is Simon Peter and after the resurrection we had a large catch of fish totaling (John 21:11) (a) 153, (b) 351, (c) 13, (d) 72, (e) the Bible does not say.

15. I wrote that there are different kinds of flesh for humans, animals, birds and fish (I Corinthians 15:39). Who am I? (a) Jesus, as recorded by Paul, (b) Simon Peter, as recorded by Paul, (c) Paul, as recorded by Paul (d) Barnabas, as recorded by Barnabas, (e) Silas, as recorded by Paul.

ANSWERS: *1 (a) God, 2 (c) Noah, 3 (b) the water becoming blood, 4 (a) Israelites, 5 (c) Solomon, 6 (d) the wall around the Temple, 7 (a) Job, 8 (b) Great Fish, 9 (c) a snake, 10 (b) two fish, 11 (d) Simon Peter, 12 (c) He had me go fishing and I found a coin in the fish's mouth, 13 (b) a piece of broiled fish, 14 (a) 153, 15 (c) Paul, as recorded by Paul.*

SCORING: 15 correct—Great catch. 13 or 14 correct—You didn't let many get away! 11 or 12 correct—A few got away but you did well! 10 or fewer correct—Something's a little fishy. Try again!

Flying in the Bible

(Airplanes have made our world smaller. Some of us like to fly while others do not care for this way of getting around. Does the Bible talk about "flying"? Yes and no. There are obvious references to flying and there are others to rapid movement. See if you can determine the answers to "Flying in the Bible" without checking the Biblical reference.)

1. In the creation account in Genesis 1-2 God speaks about these flying "above the earth." (Genesis 1:20) (a) Angels, (b) Birds, (c) Stars, (d) Humans, (e) none of the above.

2. In the rules about eating God's people were allowed to eat this "flying" item (Leviticus 11:21-23): (a) locust, (b) katydid, (c) cricket, (d) grasshopper, (e) all of the above, (f) none of the above.

3. The word "fly" in the King James or "pounce" in the New International Version refers to this happening during the time of Saul. (I Samuel 15:19) (a) They "flew" or "pounced" on the spoils of war, (b) they tried to jump of a mountain but failed, (c) they threw the opposing king from the top of the Temple to see if he could fly, (d) none of the above.

4. This man who later became king of Israel "flew" from his enemies and Psalm 18 speaks about his rescue from his enemies and, particularly, the first king of Israel. Who "flew" like an angel from his enemies? (II Samuel 22:11 and Psalm 18:1) (a) Saul, (b) David, (c) Asaph, (d) Solomon, (e) none of the above.

5. "Man is born to trouble," says Job, just as surely as this flies upwards. According to Job, what flies? (Job 5:7) (a) Eagles, (b) Crows, (c) Hawks, (d) Sparks, (e) Prayers, (f) none of the above.

6. When he talks to Job the man Zophar says that this "flies away" no more to be found (Job 20:8): (a) Dream, (b) Thief, (c) Scoundrel, (d) Eagle, (e) None of the above.

7. In one of his songs David says that he wishes he could have wings and "fly away" like this (Psalm 55:6): (a) Chaff, (b) Dove, (c) Betrayer, (d) Grasshopper, (e) None of the above.

8. In lamenting about the reality of death and dying in this Psalm Moses says that we all do this: (Psalm 90:10): (a) we all fly away, (b) we all appear before God's judgment, (c) we all fly to the grave, (d) we all fly to our mother's arms, (e) none of the above.

9. According to Psalm 91 we do not have to fear the terror of the night nor this which flies by day. (Psalm 91:5) (a) Eagle, (b) Lightning, (c) Arrow, (d) Clouds, (e) none of the above.

10. The writer of the book of Proverbs says that when we look at this it "flies away." What is he referring to? (Proverbs 23:5) (a) Eagles, (b) Wrens, (c) Riches, (d) Friends, (e) None of the above.

11. In his Temple vision this flew to Isaiah carrying a hot coal. What was it? (Isaiah 6:6) (a) Seraphim, (b) Crow, (c) Sparrow, (d) Dove, (e) Burning firepot.

12. In the same Temple vision in Isaiah 6 God describes the living beings who were flying as having this number of wings. (Isaiah 6:2) (a) Two, (b) Four, (c) Six, (d) Eight, (e) None.

13. As Isaiah describes some visions of the coming Messiah who is Jesus, he asks questions about what is "flying" along like clouds in celebration of the coming Christ. He compares it with this. (Isaiah 60:8) (a) Seraphim, (b) Crow, (c) Sparrow, (d) Dove, (e) Tongs.

14. Jeremiah wrote about this cruel nation that produced one of the ancestors of David. He writes that God would swoop and fly down like an eagle and destroy this evil

land. Name the land. (Jeremiah 48:40) (a) Moab, (b) Israel, (c) Egypt, (d) Edom, (e) none of the above.

15. From a windstorm Ezekiel saw these items moving and flying along with beings with faces of a man, a lion, an ox, and an eagle. What were these items? (a) Wheels, (b) Helicopters, (c) Chariots, (d) Wagons, (e) none of the above.

16. This angelic being appeared to Daniel at the time of the evening prayer "in swift flight." What was the angel's name? (Daniel 9:21) (a) Michael, (b) Lucifer, (c) Gabriel, (d) Melchizedek.

17. This possession of Ephraim (a descendant of Joseph) will "fly away" because of its punishment for sin. (Hosea 9:11) (a) Glory, (b) Fame, (c) Money, (d) People, (e) none of the above.

18. The prophet Habakkuk complains to God and asks questions about why evil is not eradicated. God compares His judgment with something that flies like this. (Habakkuk 1:8) (a) Crow, (b) Angel, (c) Vulture, (d) Spear, (e) Seagull.

19. In an unusual vision Zechariah saw this item flying. (Zechariah 5:1-2) (a) Building, (b) Scroll, (c) Tree, (d) Javelin, (e) none of the above.

20. One of the living creatures in the book of Revelation (Revelation 4:7) (a) resembled a lion, (b) resembled an ox, (c) resembled a human being, (d) resembled a flying eagle, (e) all of the above.

ANSWERS: (1) b/Birds; (2) e/all of the above; (3) a/They "flew" or "pounced" on the spoils of war; (4) b/David; (5) d/Sparks; (6) a/Dream; (7) b/Dove; (8) a/we all fly away; (9) c/Arrow; (10) c/Riches; (11) a/Seraphim; (12) d/Six; (13) d/Dove; (14) a/Moab; (15) a/Wheels; (16) c/Gabriel; (17) a/Glory; (18) c/Vulture; (19) b/Scroll; (20) e/all of the above.

SCORING: 18-19 correct – You soar with the Eagles; 16-17 correct – You are comfortable on both land and in the air; 14-15 correct – You need a few more flight lessons; Less than 15 correct – "Fly" back to the pages of the Bible and check your concordance.

Food in the Bible

(When we think of Thanksgiving we almost always think about food, one of the basic parts of our existence. Our Thanksgiving meals often include turkey, mashed potatoes, vegetables, cranberries, bread, pumpkin pie and other goodies. Many of the Thanksgiving foods were not available in Bible times but the blessings of food were part of life and living for God's people. Take this quiz on food in the Bible and find new things for which to be thankful.)

1. The food that Adam and Eve sinfully ate in the Garden of Eden (Genesis 3:6) was (a) an apple, (b) a pear, (c) a pomegranate, (d) not identified, (e) none of the above.

2. Abraham welcomed three men to his tent and he provided the following foods (Genesis 18:6-8) except for (a) curds, (b) milk, (c) calf, (d) bread, (e) leeks.

3. When God's people complained that they didn't have meat in the wilderness and only manna they thought of the following foods from the time they were in Egypt (Numbers 11:6) except for (a) fish, (b) cucumbers, (c) melons, (d) leeks, (e) onions, (f) garlic, (g) none of the above.

4. God's people were ready to enter the Promised Land after 40 years in the wilderness. Which of the following foods did God promise to His people (Deuteronomy 8:7-12)? (a) wheat, (b) barley, (c) figs, (d) olives, (e) honey, (f) bread, (g) all of the above.

5. In order to rescue her foolish husband, Nabal, the woman Abigail (I Samuel 25:18) presented the following foods to David and his men in the wilderness except for (a) wine, (b) leeks, (c) sheep, (d) raisins, (e) figs.

6. One of the blessings of eternal life with the Lord was (Isaiah 55:1) (a) eating only bread forever, (b) not having

to eat at all, (c) buying wine and milk without money, (d) eating steak and potatoes in heaven, (e) none of the above.

7. When asked about food while in the Babylonian captivity Daniel requested that in order to stay healthy he and the other young Jewish men (Daniel 1:12) eat only (a) vegetables and water, (b) cheese and crackers, (c) bread and wine, (d) all of the above, (e) none of the above.

8. The unusual eating habits of John the Baptist (Matthew 3:4) included eating (a) figs, (b) pomegranates, (c) pork, (d) liver, (e) none of the above.

9. In the Bible accounts of the Passover which became Jesus' Last Supper the following foods are mentioned in the Bible (Matthew 26:26-29): (a) bread, (b) wine, (c) lamb, (d) vegetables, (e) all of the above, (f) only a and b.

10. In talking about food Jesus said (John 4:34), (a) we should not eat with tax collectors and sinners, (b) His food was to do the will of God, (c) we should sit in the seat of honor when invited to a meal, (d) being hungry and thirsty is part of being a Christian.

11. In one of his resurrection appearances Jesus appeared to seven of his disciples and enjoyed eating with them (John 21:13) (a) cheese and manna, (b) figs and pomegranates (c) bread and fish, (d) raisins and sweet bread, (e) none of the above.

12. The author of the book of Hebrews (13:2) talks of the importance of entertaining people with a meal because (a) by so doing we could entertain angels without knowing it, (b) the poor need food too, (c) God will punish those who don't share, (d) we don't want to be like the rich man in the story of Lazarus.

ANSWERS: *(1) d-not identified, (2) e-leeks, (3) g-none of the above, (4) g-all of the above, (5) b-leeks, (6) c-buying wine and milk without money, (7) a-vegetables and water, (8) e-none of the above, (9) f-only a and b, (10) b-His food was to do the will of God, (11) c-bread and fish, (12) a-by so doing we could entertain angels without knowing it.*

SCORING: 12 correct--Excellent! Give thanks for His Word! 11-10 correct—Continue to taste and see that the Lord is good. 9-8 correct—Keep chewing away on the pages of the Bible. 7 or fewer—Are you hungry for more?

Fools in the Bible

(Each April 1 we "celebrate" April Fool's Day. The idea of "fools" occurs from time to time in the pages of the Bible and suggests a little quiz on fools. Select the correct response concerning the "Fools In the Bible." If you need help with the questions, consider the Biblical reference. If the verse would foolishly give away the answer only the passage is giving and not the name of the book. I'm no fool!)

1. My name is Samuel and I was a priest and prophet and judge. I scolded this king and said that he acted foolishly when he offered sacrifice when he was not to do so (I Samuel 13:13). Who was this king? (a) Samson, (b) Eli, (c) Saul, (d) David, (e) Absalom.

2. My husband, Nabal (whose name suggests the idea of fool) was a fool indeed for being rude to King David, my future husband. What is my name? (I Samuel 25:25) (a) Ruth, (b) Naomi, (c) Abigail, (d) Michal, (e) Bathsheba.

3. I was the King of Israel and when my general, Abner, was killed in a cunning act of vengeance I lamented and asked why he should die as "fools" (or lawless people) die?! (II Samuel 3:33). Why indeed! Who am I? (a) David, (b) Solomon, (c) Josiah, (d) Zedekiah.

4. The Bible says that despite my great losses of children, wealth, and health, I did not foolishly question God (chapter 1:22). What is my name? (a) Isaiah, (b) Jeremiah, (c) Ezekiel, (d) Job.

5. I wrote, "Answer a fool according to his folly" and "Answer not a fool according to his folly." (Proverbs 26:4-5) Who am I? (a) David (b) Solomon, (c) Rehoboam, (d) Jesus.

6. In my prophecy in Zechariah chapter 11 as a prophet I spoke for God and used this imagery: (a) foolish shepherds, (c) foolish prophets, (c) foolish kings, (d) foolish angels.

7. My name is Jesus and in one of my sermons (Matthew 7:26) I said that the foolish man built his house on this. (a) Clay, (b) Sand, (c) Rock, (d) Timber.

8. My name is Jesus and I called these individuals "blind fools" in a scathing series of seven woes (Matthew 23:17). Who were these fools? (a) Samaritans, (b) Pharisees, (c) Essenes, (d) Priests.

9. In speaking about idolatry in Romans 1:21-23 I, the Apostle Paul, wrote that sinful humans became fools and exchanged the glory of God for (a) images of mortal man, (b) images of birds, (c) images of animals, (d) images of reptiles, (e) all of the above.

10. In I Corinthians 1:20 I, Paul, wrote that God has made foolish the wisdom of (a) kings, (b) scholars, (c) princes, (d) the world.

11. I, Paul, wrote that this group of people (chapter 3:1) are "foolish" because they gave up the freedoms that they had in Christ. Who were these people? (a) Thessalonians, (b) Colossians, (c) Galatians, (d) Ephesians.

12. In one of my messages I, Jesus, said that "folly" (or foolishness) comes out of this (Mark 7:21-23). (a) Stomach, (b) Heart, (c) Throat, (d) Speech.

13. My name is Peter and I wrote that by doing good we can silence this kind of talk in foolish men (I Peter 2:15): (a) ignorant, (b) lying, (c) sassy, (d) hypocritical.

14. On one occasion I, Jesus, told this parable of five wise and five foolish beings (Matthew 25:2). What were these beings? (a) Men, (b) Young Women, (c) Sheep, (d) Birds.

15. In one of my letters to Titus, I, Paul, urged him and his readers to avoid these foolish things (Titus 3:9) (a) controversies, (b) genealogies, (c) arguments, (d) quarrels about the law (e) all of the above.

ANSWERS: (1) c, (2) c, (3) a, (4) d, (5) b, (6) a, (7) b, (8) b, (9) e, (10) d, (11) c, (12) b, (13) a, (14) b, (15) e.

Pastor Willis Schwichtenberg

SCORING: 15-14 correct – You are no fool; you have answered correctly; 12-13 correct – As we study God's Word we become fools for Christ!; 11 or fewer correct – It would be wise to study the Bible even more!

Freedom in the Bible

(On July 4, our nation celebrates its freedom and independence. The Bible has many references to freedom. This Independence Day "quiz" see if you can name the freedom-related Biblical character or situation being described. If you need help, check the Bible reference. In the case of the prophetic books the help is not given because the answer is the same as the Biblical book.)

1. Freedom was celebrated in a year-long observance to be observed every 50 years. Slaves were set free and property was returned to family ownership. Name this freedom year. (Leviticus 25:10-11)
2. In John 8:31-32 Jesus said we will be set free when we continue in His Word and know this word which Jesus also used to describe Himself. What is this word?
3. In order to free His people from Egyptian slavery God sent these events to show His power over the Egyptian "gods." Name these events. (Exodus 11:1)
4. Paul wrote thirteen New Testament books on a variety of subjects. What was his great book on Christian freedom?
5. When Jesus faced the governor, Pontius Pilate, this man ended up being freed instead of Jesus. Name this man. (Matthew 27:21)
6. Even though his brothers sold him into slavery this man gave his brothers their freedom when they were reunited in Egypt. Name this forgiving brother. (Exodus 50:19-20)
7. These people lost their freedom and were expelled from the Garden of Eden because God resolved to free them from their sins through His promised Messiah. Name this couple. (Genesis 3:21-24)
8. In the last verses of the Bible this Greek word is used to pray that Jesus would return. Give the Greek word or its equivalent. (Revelation 22:20)

9. This prophet freed a harlot and married her at God's insistence, however, he found that he had to "free" her again and again as she resumed her harlotry. Name this prophet.

10. This prophet was trapped inside a whale or great fish and was freed by the grace of God following a prophetic prayer. Name this reluctant prophet.

11. When the church was praying for Peter to be freed from prison the congregation would not believe this woman's report that Peter has been released. Name this woman. (Acts 12:12-17)

12. God's people lost their freedom and independence and faced captivity by this nation as an object lesson for repetance. Name this nation and captivity. (II Kings 25)

ANSWERS: (1) Jubilee, (2) Truth, (3) Ten Plagues, (4) Galatians, (5) Barabbas, (6) Joseph, (7) Adam and Eve, (8) "Maranatha" or "Come, Lord Jesus", (9) Hosea, (10) Jonah, (11) Rhoda, (12) Babylonians; Babylonian Captivity.

SCORING: 12 or 11 correct—You know freedom and have freedom in Christ; 10 or 9 correct—Feel free to celebrate your freedoms; 8 or fewer correct; You are free to page through the Bible even more.

Gifts in the Bible

(The major holiday of December is Christmas which is also a day for traditional gift-giving. Though the Bible doesn't talk specifically about the celebration of Christmas or the exchange of gifts, there are some Biblical incidents of gifts and gift giving. Using the clues provided (and the Bible passage, if necessary) see if you can determine the person or gift or situation being described from the New Testament. If the Bible reference would give away the answer, only the number reference is given. Make no mistake about it, these "gifts" will be difficult to "open.")

1. I said, "You know how to give good gifts to your children" and used these words to remind my listeners about our Heavenly Father and His gifts. (Matthew 7:11) Who am I? (a) John the Baptist, (b) Jesus, (c) Matthew, (d) Paul

2. In the Christmas story we were individuals who were not kings but we did present gifts to the newborn Christ child. (Matthew 2:11) Who are we? (a) Innkeeper, (b) Joseph, (c) Mary, (d) Magi, (e) none of the above

3. I wrote that we are saved by grace alone which is a gift of God and not because of works. (Ephesians 2:8). Who am I? (a) Paul, (b) Jesus, (c) Peter, (d) James, (e) none of the above

4. In the book of Hebrews we are described as individuals who presented gifts at the altar and who represented the coming Christ. (Hebrews 5:1) Who are we? (a) Scribes, (b) Pharisees, (c) High Priest, (d) King

5. In writing to these people I, the Apostle Paul, said that I was not looking for a gift. (4:17) Who was I writing to? (a) Hebrews, (b) Corinthians, (c) Thessalonians, (d) Philippians

6. I wrote that every good gift comes down from above and from the father of heavenly lights. (1:17) Who am I? (a) James, (b) Jesus, (c) Jude, (d) John

7. As the children of Israel sometimes we designated this as a gift to God and thus we did not fulfill our family duties. (Mark 7:11) Give the name of this obscure gift. (a) Levite, (b) Denarii, (c) Corban, (d) Shekel

8. I, the Apostle Paul, wrote to these people in a faraway country that I wanted to impart to them some kind of spiritual gift. (1:11) Who were these people? (a) Rome, (b) London, (c) Istanbul, (d) Tyre, (d) Sidon

9. I, the Apostle Peter, wrote that people should use their gifts in order to do this. (I Peter 4:10) What did I say that they should do with their gifts? (a) give it to church, (b) give it to the poor, (c) use it to serve, (d) bury it for later use

10. Since this group of churches was very messed up in how it understood spiritual gifts I had to write two letters to them and include many chapters and references to their problem. (7:7, 12:4, 12:9, 13:1-13) What was the name of these congregations? (a) Laodiceans, (b) Corinthians, (c) Thessalonians, (d) Galatians

11. When we looked at the Temple we were very impressed with the beautiful stones and the gifts dedicated to God. (Luke 21:5) Who are we? (a) Pharisees, (b) Sadducees, (c) Disciples, (d) Essenes

12. Paul wrote about us and how God gave us gifts. The word describing us would match the phrase referring to us as Babylonian exiles. It would describe our situation. (Ephesians 4:8) Who are we? (a) Free men, (b) Captives, (c) Wise men, (d) Apostles

13. On Pentecost Sunday as I preached a sermon I assured the people that as they repented and were baptized they would receive the "gift" of the Holy Spirit. (Acts 2:38) Who am I? (a) Jesus, (b) Paul, (c) Barnabas, (d) Peter, (e) James

14. I tried to buy the gifts that the apostles were sharing with the people when signs and wonders were happening in Jerusalem. My name is now used to describe purchasing

religious favors. (Acts 8:9-20) Who am I? (a) Simon Magnus, (b) Simon Peter, (c) Simon of Cyrene, (d) Simon Zealotes, (e) Simon the Canaanite

15. We were the recipients of the gift of God's grace when the Apostle Peter saw a special vision from heaven in Joppa. (Acts 11:17-18) Who are we? (a) Judeans, (b) Gentiles, (c) Asians, (d) Joppeans, (e) Canaanites

ANSWERS: *(1) b-Jesus, (2) d-Magi, (3) a-Paul, (4) c-High Priest, (5) d-Philippians, (6) a-James, (7) c-Corban, (8) a-Rome, (9) c-use it to serve, (10) b-Corinthians, (11) c-Disciples, (12) b-Captives, (13) d-Peter, (14) a-Simon Magnus, (15) b-Gentiles*

SCORING: 15 or 14 correct—You have a gift; 12-13 Correct—You should be teaching Sunday School, 11-10 correct—Not bad; your gift is helpfulness, 9-8 correct—Your gift is on hold; 7 or Less Correct—Join the club!

Hair in the Bible

(Hair played a prominent role in the life of many Biblical characters and in many Biblical situations. Supply the answer to these statements about "hair." Check the reference if you need help. Some Bible book references are not given because they would give away the answer!)

_____ 1. This Biblical book gave rules for cutting hair that were especially important for certain groups of God's covenant people (19:27).

_____ 2. This woman anointed the hair of Jesus with oil (Mark 14:3).

_____ 3. Once a year was enough for this man to cut his hair (II Samuel 14:25-26).

_____ 4. In many places in this book of songs and praises gray hair is seen as a token of wisdom and experience.

_____ 5. This Old Testament writer spoke of how he pulled out hair because of the abuses of God's people (13:25).

_____ 6. Sampson was tricked by this woman but her helpers, not she, cut his hair (Judges 16:19).

_____ 7. These individuals took vows not to cut their hair as part of an expression to glorify God (Numbers 6:1, 5).

_____ 8. This man's hair grew long and he ate grass like an ox as part of God-induced insanity (Daniel 4:33).

_____ 9. This man showed God's care and concern by preaching that even the hairs of our heads are "numbered" (Matthew 10:33).

_____ 10. This man was said to have had a hairy body and thus his brother was able to trick their aged father by using an animal skin to assume his twin's identity (Genesis 27:22-23).

ANSWERS: *(1) Leviticus, (2) Mary of Bethany, (3) Absalom, David's son, (4) Psalms, (5) Nehemiah, (6) Delilah, (7) Nazirites, (8) Nebuchadnezzar, (9) Jesus, (10) Esau.*

SCORING: 10 correct: You have a full "head" of hair, so to speak; 9 correct: As Jesus said, "Even the hairs on your head are numbered; 8 correct: Don't part with your study of the Word; Fewer than 8 correct: Long for more study of the Word!

Happiness and Sadness in the Bible

(Happiness (Joy) and sadness are both Biblical themes. As we know, there is even joy in the midst of sadness, as in the case of the death and resurrection of our Savior, Jesus Christ, and the death of those who by faith are on their way to heaven and eternity. Following the "clues" given, determine the Biblical character or people described as being "happy" or "sad." Check the Biblical reference if you need more help.)

1. I wept at the grave of my friend, Lazarus. Who am I? *(John 11:35)* (a) Jesus, (b) Mary, (c) Martha, (d) all of the above.
2. I was happy over the birth of a son at age 100. Who am I? *(Genesis 21:5)* (a) Adam, (b) Noah, (c) Abraham, (d) Zechariah.
3. I was sad about a plant's death? Who am I? *(Jonah 1:7-9)* (a) Joshua, (b) David, (c) Barnabas, (d) Jonah.
4. I was happy to bear the son of God. Who am I? *(Luke 1:30, 46-47)* (a) Mary Magdalene, (b) Mary of Bethany, (c) Mary, wife of Joseph, (d) Mary, mother of James and Joses.
5. I was sad about deceiving my brother but happy upon our reconciliation. Who am I? *(Genesis 33:4)* (a) Esau, (b) Jacob, (c) Abraham, (d) Moses.
6. We expressed our joy in heavenly songs at the birth of God's son. Who are we? *(Luke 2:13-15)* (a) Shepherds, (b) Wise Men, (c) Innkeeper, (d) Angels.
7. I was sad at the death of my son, born out of an adulterous relationship with the wife of one of my soldiers. Who am I? *(II Samuel 12:16-18)* (a) Moses, (b) Joshua, (c) David, (d) Ahaz.
8. I expressed my joy at the birth of God's son by saying I was ready to die. Who am I? *(Luke 2:28-30)* (a) Joseph, (b) Zebedee, (c) Simeon, (d) Zechariah.

9. I was sad that my mother-in-law was very ill, but happy over a miracle performed by Jesus. Who am I? *(Matthew 8:14ff.)* (a) Simon Peter, (b) Simon the Leper, (c) Simon the Zealot, (d) Simon the Canaanite.

10. I was joyful at the birth of the first child in the world. Who am I? *(Genesis 4:1)* (a) Adam, (b) Eve, (c) God, (d) all of the above.

11. I was sad that my people complained about manna but happy that Moses interceded for them. Who am I? *(Exodus 16)* (a) Paul, (b) Peter, (c) God, (d) Timothy.

12. Paul, was happy over the faith and support of these New Testament people. Name these people. *(Philippians 1:3)* (a) Philippians, (b) Galatians, (c) Ephesians, (d) Corinthians, (e) none of the above.

13. I was sad that one group of people in Asia were neither hot nor cold in their faith. I threatened to "spew" them out of my mouth. Who am I? *(Revelation 1:2, 3:15)* (a) Paul, (b) Peter, (c) Jude, (d) God.

14. I said, "Blessed" or "Happy" are those who hear the Word of God and keep it. Who am I? *(Luke 11:28)* (a) Paul, (b) Jesus, (c) Timothy, (d) Moses.

15. I was sad that my son was killed, even though he was a disrespectful traitor to my throne. Who am I? *(II Samuel 19:1-4)* (a) Absalom, (b) Solomon, (c) David, (e) Jeroboam.

ANSWERS: *(1) d/All of the Above, (2) c/Abraham, (3) d/Jonah, (4) c/ Mary, wife of Joseph, (5) b/ Jacob, (6) d/Angels, (7) c/David, (8) c/Simeon, (9) a/Peter, (10) d/All of the above, (11) c/God, (12) a/Philippians, (13) d/ God, (14) b/Jesus, (15) a/David*

SCORING: 14 or 15 correct – You must joyfully teach Sunday School!; 12 or 13 correct – You happily know your Bible pretty well; 10 or 11 – OK, but why are you frowning?; Less than 10 correct – Don't forget the sad part of this quiz!

Holy Week in the Bible

(The week before Easter the Christian Church observes what is called "Holy Week." It begins with the events of Palm Sunday and the triumphant entry of Jesus into Jerusalem, includes the cleansing of the Temple and a variety of teachings by Jesus during the coming days, the institution of the Lord's Supper on "Holy Thursday" which is sometimes called "Mandate Thursday" or "Maundy Thursday," the arrest and trial of Jesus and His death and burial on Good Friday. Some of these events are covered in this Bible quiz. See if you can determine the answers without checking the Biblical reference.)

1. Jesus came into Jerusalem on the day we call Palm Sunday riding on a donkey. A similar event in the Old Testament (I Kings 1:38-40) involved (a) Solomon (b) Abraham, (c) Moses, (d) Judah, son of Jacob, (e) none of the above.

2. The word "Hosanna" that the people and children cried as Jesus came into Jerusalem (Matthew 21:9) means (a) Hail, Caesar, (b) Lord, save us, (c) We are happy indeed, (d) Get rid of the Romans, (e) none of the above.

3. When Jesus "cleansed the Temple" on Sunday or Monday (Matthew 21:12-13) He (a) overturned the money changer's tables, (b) said that God's house should be "a house of prayer," (c) overturned benches of dove sellers (d) said that the people were making the Temple into a "den of robbers," (e) all of the above.

4. All of the following are true about the anointing of Jesus in Bethany during holy week (Mark 14:1-9) except (a) the event happened in the home of Simon the Leper, (b) the perfume she used was pure nard, (c) Jesus' feet were anointed, (d) complaints about a waste of perfume were made, (e) none of the above.

5. At the Last Supper with His disciples on Thursday Jesus (John 13) (a) washed His disciples feet, (b) predicted His

betrayal, (c) predicted Simon Peter's denial, (d) all of the above, (e) none of the above.

6. At the Passover observance with His disciples this cup of wine (I Corinthians 10:16) was used by Jesus as the basis for Holy Communion: (a) cup of freedom, (b) cup of salvation, (c) cup of blessing/thanksgiving, (d) cup of praise.

7. The place at which Jesus prayed after the Last Supper on Thursday of Holy Week (Matthew 26:30, 36) was called (a) Mount of Olives, (b) Gethsemane, (c) Mount Calvary, (d) Both "a" and "b" (d) None of the above, (e) All of the above.

8. At Gethsemane as Jesus prayed He asked the following to go with Him for prayer (Mark 14:32-33): (a) Matthew, Luke and John, (b) Peter, James and John, (c) Andrew, Peter and James, (d) Philip, Thomas and Peter.

9. All of the men named Judas listed below are in the Bible but the man who betrayed Jesus with a kiss (Luke 22:3-6, 47-48) had the name (a) Judas Thaddeus, (b) Judas Barsabbas, (c) Judas Iscariot, (d) Judas Maccabeus, (e) Judas the Galilean.

10. In separate "trials" Jesus appeared before (John 18:12-40), (a) Annas, (b) Caiaphas, (c) Pontius Pilate, (d) Herod, (e) All of the above except "a", (f) All of the above.

11. Instead of releasing Jesus in following a Passover Festival custom (Luke 23:18-25) Pontius Pilate ordered that the following Biblical person be released: (a) Barnabas, (b) Barabbas, (c) Barsabbas, (d) Bartimaeus, (e) Bartholomew.

12. A compilation of the four Gospels shows that Jesus spoke from the cross on Good Friday (Luke 23:34-46, Mark 15:34, John 19:26-30) a total of (a) Three times, (b) Four times, (c) Seven times, (d) Ten times, (e) none of the above.

ANSWERS: *(1) a/Solomon; (2) b/Lord, save us; (3) e/all of the above; (4) c/Jesus' feet were anointed; (5) d/all of the above; (6) c/Cup of blessing/*

thanksgiving; (7) d/both "a" and "b"; (8) b/Peter, James and John; (9) c/ Judas Iscariot; (10) f/all of the above; (11) b/Barabbas; (12) c/Seven times.

SCORING: 12 correct – You know what's going on next week; 11 or 10 correct – You are with Jesus at this difficult time; 9 or fewer correct – Spend some quiet time with Jesus and the Word during this coming "Holy Week".

Horses in the Bible

(Horses are mentioned in many places in the Bible with both actual and figurative references. Horses are often mentioned in prophetic and poetic books and are often associated with war and power. Using the Biblical clues given, see if you can determine the thoughts about the horses which are described or the people involved in various Biblical references to horses. If you need help, you may wish to check the Bible passage.)

1. I am a horse. Because I was/am a land animal and in modern parlance, a mammal, can you name the day of creation on which God made me? (Genesis 1:24-25) (a) Second Day, (b) Third day, (c) Fourth day, (d) Fifth day, (e) Sixth day.

2. I am the Pharaoh of the Exodus and after the tenth plague and the children of Israel were gone I had my horsemen and chariots pursue them. Can you name how many horses and chariots I sent? (Exodus 14:6-7) (a) More than 600, (b) 400, (c) 200, (d) 39, (e) None of the above.

3. We sang a song which included a line about horses after Pharaoh's soldiers and their chariots were lost in the Red Sea. Can you name me and the song which bears my name that God's people sang? (Exodus 15:1) (a) Moses, (b) Joshua, (c) Miriam, (d) Aaron.

4. I prayed to God to open the eyes of his servant to see horses and chariots of fire and to strike the enemy with blindness. What is my name? (II Kings 6:15-19) (a) Elijah, (b) Isaiah, (c) Jeremiah, (d) Elisha, (e) None of the above.

5. In defeating the Syrians God performed a miracle involving horses. What was the miracle? (II Kings 7:5-7) (a) A single horse was used to defeat the enemy, (b) God caused the Syrians to hear the sound of horses and they were filled with fear, (c) All the horses owned by the

Syrians died as a result of a plague, (d) The Syrian horses all ran away.

6. When I died after a plot by my own nation my body was brought to Jerusalem on horses and there I was buried. What is my name? (II Kings 14:19-20) (a) David, (b) Solomon, (c) Jeroboam, (d) Amaziah.

7. My name is Nehemiah. When the Jerusalem wall was repaired under my guidance one of the gates repaired was called by what horse related name? Can you name it? (Nehemiah 3:20) (a) Pony Gate, (b) Horse Gate, (c) Colt Gate, (d) Mane Gate.

8. According to one of the Psalms I, the Lord, delight in something. What is it? (Psalm 147:10) (a) The beauty of horses, (b) The number of horses, (c) The strength of horses, (d) The wisdom of horses.

9. My name is Joel and God revealed to me that certain creatures were like horses marching. What were these marching creatures? (Joel 2:4) (a) Frogs, (b) Locusts, (c) Storks, (d) Mice, (e) Flies.

10. My name is Zechariah and I had a vision of different colored horses and a man riding on one of them. Can you name the color of the horse on which I was riding? (Zechariah 1:7) (a) Black, (b) Pale (c) Red, (d) Mottled.

11. I wrote much about horses and in my prophecy about the Messiah entering Jerusalem. In this same prophecy I said that this would be "cut off." What animal was I talk about? (Zechariah 9:10) (a) Dead horse, (b) White horse, (c) Plain horse, (d) War horse.

12. My name is Jesus and when I entered Jerusalem on what you call "Palm Sunday" I rode into the city on what kind of beast or beasts? (Matthew 21:1-5) (a) Donkey and colt, (b) White horse, (c) White horse and a pale horse, (d) A gray horse, (e) None of the above.

13. My name is James and I talked in my New Testament epistle about a bit in the mouth of a horse. Do you remember what I said? (James 3:3) (a) Avoid eating any

meat of animals controlled by bits, (b) Bits in the mouths of horses cause them to obey us, (c) We cannot control two horses with one bit, (d) None of the above.

14. My name is John and in the prophecy given to me in the book of Revelation all of the following horses are name except for what horse? (Revelation 6:2-8) (a) White, (b) Red, (c) Black, (d) Pale, (e) All of the above, (f) None of the above.

15. In my Revelation vision, I, John, saw a white horse with a person sitting on it. The following words describe the person sitting on this horse (Revelation 19:11-13) (a) Is called faithful and true, (b) Judges and makes war, (c) Has eyes like a flame of fire, (d) Is clothed in a robe dipped in blood, (e) All of the above, (f) none of the above.

ANSWERS: (1) e-Sixth day, (2) a-More than 600, (3) a-Moses, (4) d-Elisha, (5) b-God caused the Syrians to hear the sound of horses and they were filled with fear, (6) d-Amaziah, (7) b-Horse gate, (8) c-The strength of horses, (9) b-Locusts, (10) c-Red, (11) d-War horse, (12) a-Donkey and colt, (13) b-Bits in the mouths of horses cause them to obey us, (14) f-None of the above, (15) e-All of the above.

SCORING: 15-14 Correct-Giddy up and go! You have done great! 13-12 Correct-You have done well; no need to ride off into the sunset, 11-10 Correct-Check the stable for more answers, 9 or fewer correct-Perhaps you need to explore a horse of a different color.

I Am Thankful

(When you consider Thanksgiving Day, for what are you thankful? Many of the Old Testament heroes, patriarchs and matriarchs had much to be thankful for. See if you can determine which character is being described. Use the Biblical reference if you need help.)

1. I am glad that God gave us a promise of a Savior after our sinful eating got us kicked out of the Garden of Eden. Who are we? (Genesis 3:23-24, 4:1) (a) David and Bathsheba, (b) Abraham and Sarah, (c) Adam and Eve, (d) Solomon and Sheba, (e) Moses and Zipporah

2. I am thankful that even though I killed my brother, God spared my life and gave me a protective mark. Who am I? (Genesis 4:9-16) (a) Adam, (b) Cain, (c) Abel, (d) Enoch, (e) Seth

3. I am thankful that God rescued me, my wife, my three children and their spouses during the great flood. Who am I? (Genesis 6:9, 17-18) (a) Joshua, (b) Solomon, (c) Enoch, (d) Abraham, (e) Noah

4. I am thankful that even though I laughed at the prospect of having a child in my old age, that God still kept His promise to me. Who am I? (Genesis 18:11-15) (a) Eve, (b) Sarah, (c) Rebekah, (d) Rachel, (e) Bathsheba

5. I am glad that God stopped my father from sacrificing me, his firstborn son. Who am I? (Genesis 22:9-12) (a) Isaac, (b) Ishmael, (c) Issachar, (d) Isaiah, (e) Isis

6. I am thankful that God used Abraham and His angels to rescue me and my family from a sinful city but I'm not very thankful that my wife turned back and became the "salt of the earth." Who am I? (Genesis 19:16-26) (a) Zoar, (b) Abimelech, (c) Lot, (d) Laban, (e) Marks

7. I am thankful my brothers sold me into slavery because, ultimately, it was a rescuing my family during a severe

famine. Who am I? (Genesis 50:19-20) (a) Benjamin, (b) Issachar, (c) Joseph, (d) Caleb, (e) Jacob

8. I am thankful God used me to lead His people out of Egyptian slavery. Who am I? (Exodus 3:10-11) (a) Pharaoh, (b) Moses, (c) Aaron, (d) Joshua, (e) Jeremiah

9. I warned the people that they needed to be thankful and not forget me after their stomachs were filled and they were secure in their homes. Who am I? (Deuteronomy 8:10-20) (a) Moses, (b) Baal, (c) Lord God, (d) David, (e) Ezekiel

10. I am thankful that I got to lead God's people into the Holy Land after the death of our longtime leader, Moses. Who am I? (Deuteronomy 34:9) (a) Joshua, (b) Aaron, (c) Miriam, (d) Joseph, (e) Noah

11. I am thankful that I was able to hide the Hebrew spies who were getting ready to secure the Promised Land. Who am I? (Joshua 2:1-6) (a) Sarah, (b) Rahab, (c) Hagar, (d) Haggai, (e) Zerapath

12. I am thankful that my husband, King David, married me despite our questionable first meeting and his subsequent sinful actions. Who am I? (II Samuel 11:2-4, 11:26-27) (a) Sheba, (b) Eve, (c) Rahab, (d) Miriam, (e) Bathsheba

13. It wasn't turkey but I am thankful God fed me with bread delivered by ravens. Who am I? (I Kings 17:2-4) (a) Elisha, (b) Jeremiah, (c) Ezekiel, (d) Elijah, (e) David

14. I am thankful that God kept telling my prophet husband to "buy me back" from a life of harlotry as an illustration of God's continuing mercy. Who am I? (Hosea 1:2-3, 3:1) (a) Gomer, (b) Bathsheba, (c) Sarah, (d) Leah, (e) Rebekah

15. I am thankful that God closed the mouths of lions when I was tossed into their den for disobeying an antireligious edict. Who am I? (Daniel 6:19-22) (a) Isaiah, (b) Jeremiah, (c) Ezekiel, (d) Elijah, (e) Daniel

ANSWERS: *(1) c/Adam and Eve; (2) b/Cain; (3) e/Noah; (4) b/Sarah; (5) a/Isaac; (6) c/Lot; (7) c/Joseph; (8) b/Moses; (9) c/Lord God; (10) a/Joshua; (11) b/Rahab; (12) e/Bathsheba; (13) d/Elijah; (14) a/Gomer; (15) e/Daniel*

SCORING: 15 or 14 Correct – Aren't you thankful that you took the quiz? 13 or 12 Correct – Aren't you thankful for the answers you knew? 11 or 10 Correct – Aren't you thankful that there are reference books to help us learn more about God's Word?

Inauguration in the Bible

(Every four years the third week in January includes the Inauguration of the president of the United States. What does the Bible say about "inauguration"? The word isn't really used in Scripture but kings, leaders, prophets and judges were called by God and thus inaugurated into service. See if you can tell which Biblical character is being described with the clues given. Some Bible book references do not include the book name because it would give the answer away.)

1. I was never really "inaugurated" to be a ruler over my family and my family preferred to see me as a slave rather than a ruler. However, through me God rescued my family and His people. (Genesis 50:19-21) Who am I? (a) Joseph, (b) Moses, (c) Joshua, (d) Abraham.

2. I was called but not really "inaugurated" to lead God's people out of Egypt. I appealed to God to choose someone else but God was adamant in making me His choice to deliver His people. (Exodus 3:10-11, 4:1-17) Who am I? (a) Joshua, (b) Gideon, (c) Moses, (d) Abraham.

3. I was reluctant to accept God's call to be a leader but you might say that God "fleeced" me into it and "inaugurated" my time of service. (Judges 6:14-24) Who am I? (a) Samson, (b) Gideon, (c) Barak, (d) Abimelech.

4. When I was just a child I received God's call in the middle of the night while I slept in the Temple. There was no inauguration" ceremony but I began my training as the new judge and priest in a prophetic fashion. (3:1-14) Who am I? (a) Eli, (b) Phineas, (c) Hophni, (d) Samuel.

5. Though my call was subtle and private when I was anointed to be king I was said to be a man after God's "own heart." Later I was "inaugurated" by the men of Judah. (I Samuel 16:7, II Samuel 2:4) Who am I? (a) Saul, (b) David, (c) Jonathan, (d) Absalom.

6. I was not a prophet but my inauguration as King included me riding into a town on a donkey (or mule) in a humble fashion. (I Kings 1:32-40) Who am I? (a) David, (b) Jesus, (c) Solomon, (d) Adonijah.

7. Though my call to serve is not described in the Bible my ministry as a prophet began with an "inauguration" speech in which I warned Ahab of the coming of a devastating drought. (I Kings 17:1) Who am I? (a) Elijah, (b) Isaiah, (c) Joel, (d) Elisha.

8. My call to serve from my mentor included an elaborate "inauguration" meal in which I slaughtered 12 oxen for a meal for my family and friends. (I Kings 19:19-21) Who am I? (a) Isaiah, (b) Jeremiah, (c) Ezekiel, (d) Elisha.

9. My name is obscure among the prophets but my call and "inauguration" into God's service was real. (I Kings 22:19-20) Who am I? (a) Micaiah, (b) Zedekiah, (c) Jehoshaphat, (d) Ramoth Gilead.

10. When I was called to serve in the Northern Kingdom of Israel I was a shepherd and vine dresser farmer in the Southern Kingdom of Judah. (7:14-16) Who am I? (a) Hosea, (b) Amos, (c) Joel, (d) Obadiah.

11. Though I didn't have a lengthy "inauguration" ceremony to begin my ministry of prophecy I told God's people about the coming invasion of locusts (1:1-4). Who am I? (a) Elijah, (b) Isaiah, (c) John, (d) Joel.

12. My call and "inauguration" to serve included a vision of angels and God in His temple on a throne with His flowing robe filling the temple (6:1-8) Who am I? (a) Isaiah, (b) Elijah, (c) David, (d) Jeremiah.

13. When my call to serve (or "inauguration" into the ministry) was given by God I complained that I was only a child and too young to speak but God overcame my objections. (1:6) Who am I? (a) Isaiah, (b) Jeremiah, (c) Ezekiel, (d) Amos.

14. I saw all sorts of wheels during God's lengthy "inauguration" of my ministry to the Babylonian exiles.

(1:15-21) Who am I? (a) Daniel, (b) Malachi, (c) Ezekiel, (d) Abraham.

15. My three young friends and I had no time for rich "inauguration" foods and other goodies and we did not defile our Hebrew faith or heritage in the process. It "inaugurated" our work in the realms of Babylon. (1:11-21) Who am I? (a) Daniel, (b) Hananiah, (c) Mishael, (d) Azariah, (e) all of the above.

ANSWERS: *(1) (a) Joseph, 2 (c) Moses, 3 (b) Gideon, 4 (d) Samuel, 5 (b) David, 6 (c) Solomon, 7 (a) Elijah, 8 (d) Elisha, 9 (a) Micaiah, 10 (b) Amos, 11 (d) Joel, 12 (a) Isaiah, 13 (b) Jeremiah, 14 (c) Ezekiel, 15 (e) All of the above.>*

SCORING: 15 correct—What a score! You are "inaugurated" with the "oil of gladness"! 13 or 14 correct—Perhaps you are "inaugurating" a whole series of Bible studies! 11 or 12 correct—You have placed your hand on the Bible! 10 or fewer correct—You need a little more study before you are "inaugurated" as a Bible scholar.

The "J's" Have It

(The Bible has many names which start with the letter "J." Using the list below, name the person being described in the brief clue. The quiz follows the order of Bible books. For more help, consult the Bible passage listed. If the book name would give away the answer, only the verse is given.)

Jacob	Jael	Japheth	Jeremiah	Jeroboam
Jesse	Jesus	Jethro	Jezebel	Joanna
Job	Joel	John	Jonah	Jonathan
Joseph	Joshua	Judah	Judas	Jude

1. Third Son of Noah (Genesis 5:32). _____
2. Renamed "Israel" by God (Genesis 32:28). _____

   _____

3. Sold into slavery by his brothers (Genesis 37:28).

   _____

4. Son of Jacob who was to be ancestor of the Messiah (Genesis 49:8-10). _____
5. Father in law of Moses (Exodus 4:18). _____
6. Successor of Moses (Deuteronomy 34:9.

   _____

7. Woman who killed the general Sisera (Judges 4:17-21).

   _____

8. Father of David (I Samuel 11:1, 10). _____
9. Friend of David (I Samuel 18:3). _____
10. Evil son of Solomon (I Kings 14:14-16).

    _____

11. Wife of Ahab (I Kings 21:25). _____
12. Prophet who wore a yoke (27:1-2). _____
13. Prophet who wrote about a locust plague (1:2-4).

    _____

14. Reluctant prophet swallowed by a large fish (Matthew 12:39-40). _____

15. Betrayer of Jesus (Matthew 26:47-50).

_____

16. One of the women followers of Jesus (Luke 24:10).

_____

17. Disciple Jesus "loved" (John 21:20). _____

18. Also called the "Christ" (I Corinthians 1:1).

_____

19. Supposedly, a "patient" man (James 5:11).

_____

20. Second to the last book of the Bible. _____

ANSWERS: *(1) Japheth, (2) Jacob, (3) Joseph, (4) Judah, (5) Jethro, (6) Joshua, (7) Jael, (8) Jesse, (9) Jonathan, (10) Jeroboam, (11) Jezebel, (12) Jeremiah, (13) Joel, (14) Jonah, (15) Judah, (16) Joanna, (17) John, (18) Jesus, (19) Job, (20) Jude.*

SCORING: If you get 19 or 20 correct, you are really "jamming", If you get 17 or 18 correct, you are "joyous", If you get 15 or 16 correct, you might be a little "jittery", if you get less than 15 correct, your score is probably "jarring."

Jails, Jailers and Prisoners in the Bible

(Like it or not, some people end up in jail or prison. The media often gives coverage to famous or infamous individuals. In the Bible there were many people who were unjustly incarcerated but there were also individuals who found themselves in jail or prison for a reason. Using the clues given, see if you can determine the jails, the jailers, the prisoners or the prisons being described in the Biblical clues given. If you need help, you may wish to check the Bible passage.)

1. My name is Lot and I wasn't in jail or prison but I was captured and all my possessions were seized. My uncle Abraham rallied his men to rescue me from this unique imprisonment. How many men did Abraham "muster" to help me? (Genesis 14:12-16) (a) 77, (b) 318, (c) 457, (d) 7 brave men.

2. I was the prison warden in Egypt and one of my trusted prisoners was so faithful that I put him in charge of the things at the prison. Can you name my trusted prisoner? (Genesis 39:20-23) (a) Abraham, (b) Isaac, (c) Jacob, (d) Joseph.

3. My prison was a living creature in which I survived for three days. This happened because I didn't want to follow God's command to preach judgment to the city of Nineveh. What was my prison? (Jonah 1:17) (a) a dinosaur, (b) a great fish, (c) a she-bear, (d) a dragon, (e) none of the above.

4. My name is Jeremiah and because I kept warning God's people not to rebel against the threat of captivity I was put in prison for my efforts. How was my imprisonment described? (Jeremiah 37:16-17) (a) vaulted dungeon, (b) house arrest, (c) confined to my own home, (d) free to roam.

5. At the time of the fall of Jerusalem I rebelled against the king. I was taken prisoner and put in shackles, the Temple was destroyed and my sons were killed in front of me and I was blinded and taken to Babylon. What is my name? (II Kings 24:20, 25:1-7) (a) Josiah, (b) Zedekiah, (c) Nebuchadnezzar, (d) Pharaoh.

6. I was a guard but did not guard in a prison. Along with others, I was assigned by the governor of Judea to stand guard over the tomb of Jesus. Who was the leader who assigned me to do this task? (Matthew 27:65-66) (a) Caesar, (b) Pilate, (c) Augustus, (d) Herod.

7. I was not a jailer but I was an executioner assigned to fulfill a strange birthday request on the part of the king's stepdaughter. Who did I execute? (Mark 6:21-29) (a) Joseph, (b) Ahab, (c) John the Baptist, (d) Jesus.

8. I am not named in the Bible but I was a prisoner who ended up being crucified at the time of Jesus' death. No, my name was not Barabbas but I spoke some famous words as "we" were dying on the cross. What were those words? (Luke 23:42) (a) It is finished, (b) Behold your son, (c) Forgive them, (d) Remember me, (e) Weep for me.

9. The prisoners in my jail were singing songs and praising God and, as the result of an earthquake, could have escaped but did not. Because of this, I became a Christian. In what city was I the jailer? (Acts 16:12-34) (a) Ephesus, (b) Philippi, (c) Galatia, (d) Corinth.

10. My name is Paul and after I appealed to the emperor, Caesar, I was sent to journey by ship to Rome with many other prisoners. Can you name the guard who was in charge of my imprisonment? (Acts 27:1-2) (a) Agabus, (b) Publius, (c) Julius, (d) Agrippa.

11. I was a prisoner named Paul and I wrote a letter to Philemon about his runaway slave. Can you name the slave who I wanted Philemon to accept as a Christian brother? (Philemon 1:10) (a) Onesimus, (b) Epaphras, (c) Timothy, (d) Mark, (e) Demos

12. I was an angel in charge of a unique prison in a vision that John had in the book of Revelation and I imprisoned Satan for a thousand years. What is the name of the place to which I banished him? (Revelation 20:1-3) (a) Magog, (b) Armageddon, (c) Omega, (d) Abyss.

ANSWERS: *(1) b-318, (2) d-Joseph, (3) b-a great fish (4) a-vaulted dungeon, (5) b-Zedekiah, (6) b-Pilate, (7) c-John the Baptist, (8) d-Remember me, (9) b-Philippi, (10) c-Julius, (11) a-Onesimus, (12) d-Abiyss.*

SCORING: 12 Correct-Nothing "escapes" you; 11 Correct-You have guarded your knowledge well, 10 Correct-Watch out for false imprisonments, 9 or fewer correct-No, you will not have to spend time in solitary study.

Joshua and Strong and Courageous

(The words, "Be strong and courageous," are from God's words to Joshua (Joshua 1:9) as he assumed leadership of the people of Israel in the wilderness and as they prepared to cross over into the Promised Land. How much do you know about Joshua and about the work that he faced? Try this little Biblical quiz based on his life and his book and see how you fare. If you need help, check the Biblical reference.)

1. Joshua was the son of (Joshua 1:1) (a) Bathsheba, (b) Nun, (c) Abishag, (d) Deborah, (e) none of the above.
2. According to Deuteronomy 34:8 the people of Israel mourned for the following number of days (a) 40, (b) 30, (c) 20, (d) 10, (e) they were told not to mourn.
3. When Israel was ready to cross the Jordan with the Ark (Joshua 3:15-16) (a) the water stopped flowing and they crossed on dry ground like they did when they crossed the Red Sea, (b) they were commanded to build a bridge for the crossing, (c) they built a boat and crossed the Jordan in groups with the ark going first, (d) they did not have to cross the Jordan but stayed on the other side.
4. Seven nations were to be conquered by Joshua and the Israel people when they were conquering the Holy Land. These seven nations (Joshua 3:10) included all of the following except the (a) Canaanites, (b) Amorites, (c) Jebusites, (d) Hittites, (e) Philistines.
5. After entering the Promised Land the people were urged to construct a special memorial (Joshua 4:2-4) which included (a) a statue of Moses and the Ten Commandments, (b) a golden calf, (c) Twelve stones as a memorial pillar, (d) none of the above.
6. With Joshua's leadership came reaffirmation of rites and ceremonies (Joshua 5) including (a) circumcision of those who had been born in the wilderness, (b) the manna

stopping, (c) celebration of the Passover, (d) all of the above, (e) none of the above.

7. The city of Jericho was conquered by Joshua and the Israelites (Joshua 6:3-5) by (a) blowing trumpets and marching around the city once, (b) marching around the city once daily for 6 days and seven times on the seventh day with trumpets and shouts, (c) a massive earthquake on the third day of marching, (d) none of the above.

8. Israel's spies who canvassed Jericho before the city was conquered had been shielded by a woman whose family was now rescued (Joshua 6:22-25). Her name was (a) Ruth, (b) Esther, (c) Naomi, (d) Rahab, (e) Gomer.

9. Reality set in for God's people when God withheld His blessing because of disobedience involving the man named (Joshua 7:1) (a) Dathan, (b) Caleb, (c) Achan, (d) Gideon.

10. When the people of Gibeon saw the destruction of Ai (Joshua 9:3ff.) they tricked Joshua and the Israelites by (a) pretending they were from a distant country and begged to be spared, (b) hiring people from Joshua's army to fight for them, (c) gathering several tribes of people to fight against Israel as a group, (d) saying that they were from Egypt and were long-lost relatives of the Israelites.

11. In a major fight with five kings and countries (Joshua 10:12-13) God intervened in a battle at Gibeon by (a) causing the kings to fight against each other, (b) sending complete darkness so that the warriors could not see in battle, (c) causing the sun to stand still for a day so the battle could continue, (d) sending wild animals to destroy the five armies.

12. The last half of the book of Joshua describes the lands that each of the tribes received in the Promised Land (Joshua 13-24). These chapters relate the fact that (a) all of the lands were now conquered, (b) much of the land was conquered by there was still work to be done, (c) all of the lands were on the west side of the Jordan River,

(d) even the Levites would be getting territory in the Promised Land.

13. When Israel originally faced entrance to the Promised Land after the Exodus two of the twelve spies urged that the work of conquering the land begin immediately. One of these men was Joshua and the other man who received a special inheritance of Hebron (Joshua 14:6-13) was named (a) Caleb, (b) Melchizedek, (c) Manasseh, (d) Ephraim, (d) Simeon.

14. In a final speech to the people before his death Joshua (Joshua 24:14-28) said (a) put away the gods that your fathers served beyond the River and in Egypt, (b) choose this day whom you will serve, (c) You are not able to serve the Lord, for He is a holy God, (d) If you forsake the Lord and serve foreign gods, then he will turn and do you harm and consume you, (e) all of the above.

ANSWERS: *1. (b) Nun, 2. (b) 30, 3. (a) the water stopped flowing and they crossed on dry ground like they did when they crossed the Red Sea, 4. (e) Philistines, 5. (c) Twelve stones as a memorial pillar, 6. (d) all of the above, 7. (b) marching around the city once daily for 6 days and seven times on the seventh day with trumpets and shouts, 8. (d) Rahab, 9. (c) Achan, 10. (a) pretending they were from a distant country and begged to be spared, 11. (c) causing the sun to stand still for a day so the battle could continue, 12. (b) much of the land was conquered by there was still work to be done, 13. (a) Caleb, 14. (e) all of the above.*

SCORING: If you got two or less wrong, you are definitely strong and courageous. If you got 3-4 incorrect, you need to spend some time in the Promised Land. If you got 5 or more incorrect, you may wish to have the sun stand still while studying the life of Joshua!

Kings In The Bible

(Kings are often crowned in many European countries. Across the channel in Great Britain others await the crowning on a new King as a successor to Queen Elizabeth, either her son or her grandson, depending on the circumstances. Kings and Queens are not so much a part of our world today but Kings were very important in the pages of the Bible. The most important "king," of course, was and is Jesus Christ, however, in this quiz, using the list below, name the Biblical King (both good and bad) being described in the brief clue. For more help, consult the Bible passage listed.)

Ahab	Ahasuerus	Caesars	Cyrus
David	Herod	Hezekiah	Jeroboam
Josiah	Melchizedek	Nebuchadnezzar	Nineveh
Pharaoh	Saul	Solomon	Zedekiah

1. This man was king of Salem and also a mysterious high priest (Genesis 14:18). _____

2. The leaders of Egypt were not called "kings" but were known by this name (Genesis 41:1). _____

3. This king built the temple in Jerusalem (I Kings 7:52). _____

4. This king allowed his wife to talk him into stealing a vineyard (I Kings 21:1-16). _____

5. This king prayed a prayer to God and his life was extended by nearly 20 years (II Kings 20:1-7). _____

6. This man was the first king of Israel (I Samuel 10:24-27). _____

7. This was the shepherd king of the Old Testament and considered the greatest king of all. He killed Goliath when he was young (I Samuel 16:13, 17:50-54). _____

8. This king introduced the worship of idols in earnest in Israel (the Northern Kingdom area) and built Shechem as a place of residence and a center for idol worship (I Kings 12:25-31). _____

9. This was the last king of Judah (II Kings 25:1-7). _____

10. This man was the "boy king" of the Old Testament (II Chronicles 34:1-2). _____

11. This king of Persia allowed the exiled Jews to return to their homeland and rebuild the Temple (II Chronicles 36:22-23). _____

12. This king was the husband of Esther (Esther 2:16-18). _____

13. This king ate grass because of his insanity (Daniel 4:33). _____

14. This king is not named in the Bible but he led his people in prayer when words of God's judgment were preached by Jonah. In what city did this king reign? (Jonah 3:6-9). _____

15. These rulers were not called "kings" but they commanded the whole Roman empire (Luke 2:1). _____

16. This king hoped to see Jesus do a miracle for his own entertainment (Luke 23:8). _____

ANSWERS: *(1) Melchizedek, (2) Pharaoh, (3) Solomon, (4) Ahab, (5) Hezekiah, (6) Saul, (7) David, (8) Jeroboam, (9) Zedekiah, (10) Josiah, (11) Cyrus, (12) Ahasuerus, (13) Nebuchadnezzar, (14) Nineveh, (15) Caesars, (16) Herod.*

SCORING: 16 Correct: You are crowned as the king of this game; 15 Correct: Not bad; you are one step away from royalty; 14 Correct: No one is perfect; not even the King; 13 or fewer correct: It is your "divine right" to keep studying.

Leap Year in the Bible

(February 29 only appears on the calendar every four years and the year is called "Leap Year." Is "Leap Year" mentioned in the Bible? Not really, but once in a while we find "leaping" references. Take this little Leap Year quiz and see if you can determine who or what is leaping. Use the Biblical reference if you need help. Ready? Set! Let's leap into this quiz.)

1. The word "leap" is not used in the story of my life but I "leaped" (leapt) over my older brother and received God's promises. (Genesis 27:36) Who am I? (a) Lot, (b) Esau, (c) Jacob, (d) Isaac.

2. I was watching the Ark of the Covenant coming into town and I saw my husband, David, the king, dancing and leaping in the royal procession. The Bible says I "despised him in my heart." (II Samuel 6:16) Who am I? (a) Michal, (b) Bathsheba, (c) Abigail, (d) Salome, (e) none of the above.

3. I was one of Job's friends who criticized him and who suggested that it was his sin which was causing all of his problems. I was later rebuked by God for my words but I did write that "my heart pounds and leaps from its place." (Job 37:1) Who am I? (a) Satan, (b) Solomon, (c) Elihu, (d) Abraham, (e) Daniel.

4. I also spoke in the book of Job and admonished his friends and asked who makes the horse "leap like a locust." (Job 39:20) Who am I? (a) Satan, (b) Job, (c) Elihu, (d) God, (e) Abraham.

5. I wrote dozens and dozens of Psalms and in Psalm 28:7 I wrote that "my heart leaps for joy, and with my song I praise Him." Who am I? (a) Amminadab, (b) David, (c) Daniel, (d) Malachi, (e) Moses.

6. There are many images about unusual objects moving and reacting in a variety of ways. In Psalm 29:6 this "leaps like

a calf." What is it? (a) Grasshopper, (b) Chicken, (c) Young man, (d) Lebanon, (e) all of the above.

7. I am called the "Rose of Sharon" and in the narrative in the Song of Solomon (2:8) I note that this leaps across the mountain: (a) my lover, (b) the sun, (c) the moon, (d) the stars, (e) all of the above.

8. My name is Isaiah and in my narrative about the joy of the redeemed I wrote (Isaiah 35:6) that (a) the lame will leap like a deer, (b) the mute tongue will shout for joy, (c) water will gush forth in the wilderness, (d) streams will run in the desert, (e) all of the above.

9. The Bible says that I "leaped to my feet" when I looked into the fiery furnace and saw four men in the flames instead of three (Daniel 3:24). My name is (a) Belshazzar, (b) Daniel, (c) Nebuchadnezzar, (d) Cyrus, (e) none of the above.

10. My name is Joel and I wrote in Joel 2:5 that these had the noise of chariots that "leap over the mountaintops" and "like a mighty army." What was I talking about? (a) Horses running, (b) Grasshoppers or locusts, (c) donkeys, (d) pigs stampeding.

11. I leaped in my mother's womb when I heard the greeting of my mother's cousin (Luke 1:41-44). Who am I? (a) John, (b) Jesus, (c) Saul, later named Paul, (d) Mary, (e) Elizabeth.

12. I told some people that when they were persecuted they should "leap for joy." (Luke 6:23) Who am I? (a) Saul, later named Paul, (b) John the Baptist, (c) Jesus, (d) Peter, (e) John the Apostle.

ANSWERS: *(1) c-Jacob, (2) a-Michal, (3) c-Elihu, (4) d-God, (5) b-David, (6) d-Lebanon, (7) a-my lover, (8) e-all of the above, (9) c-Nebuchadnezzar, (10) b-Grasshoppers or locusts, (11) a-John, (12) c-Jesus.*

Pastor Willis Schwichtenberg

SCORING: 12 correct – Jump or leap for joy about a perfect score! 10-11 correct – You are able to leap tall challenges! 9 correct – Though not perfect, you leap well! 8 or fewer correct – What can I say? Next time, look up the passage before you leap at the answer!

Leaves in the Bible

(With the advent of Autumn we see leaves changing color and falling from the trees. The Bible has some things to say about leaves. See if you can guess the incidents about leaves being described by using the clue which is given or by checking the Bible reference. If the name of the book would give the answer away the book is not named.)

1. These individuals sewed fig leaves together for covering (Genesis 3:7) (a) Jacob and Rachel, (b) Noah and his wife, (c) Adam and Eve, (d) Mary and Martha.
2. When Noah sent the dove out from the Ark a second time the dove brought back this kind of leaf in its beak (Genesis 8:11) (a) fig, (b) olive, (c) apple, (c) pine.
3. Folding leaves were part of the construction of this object by King Solomon. What was being constructed (I Kings 6:33-34)? (a) Solomon's palace, (b) Urim and Thummin, (c) Temple, (d) Tabernacle.
4. In contrasting the wicked with the righteous the Psalmist writes (Psalm 1:3) (a) the righteous is like a tree planted by streams of water, (b) the righteous tree yields its fruit in season, (c) the leaf on the righteous tree does not wither, (d) everything that the righteous tree does prospers, (e) all of the above.
5. Name the unfaithful city described in Isaiah 1:30. (a) Jerusalem, (b) Babylon, (c) Shiloh, (d) Jericho.
6. In a vision of judgment on the nations this prophet spoke about leaves falling from the vine and fig tree and the skies rolling up like a scroll (34:4). Who was this prophet? (a) Hosea, (b) Joel, (c) Isaiah, (d) Amos
7. According to Ezekiel 47:12 the leaves in the spiritual Temple in Jerusalem will not (a) be edible (b) wither, (c) turn colors, (d) produce fruit.

8. This great king in Daniel 4:12-14 saw visions of a tree with beautiful leaves and the tree itself bore food for all and provided protection for birds and animals. Who was this great king? (a) Herod, (b) Solomon, (c) Nebuchadnezzar, (d) Caesar.

9. Jesus said that when the fig trees sprout leaves (Luke 21:30) you can see for yourselves that (a) winter is near, (b) summer is near, (c) the fruit is ripe, (d) the world is ending.

10. The leaves of this tree in Revelation 22:2 are for the healing of the nation. What tree is being described? (a) Tree of Life, (b) Tree of Knowledge of Good and Evil, (c) Tree of Jerusalem, (d) Tree of Babylon.

ANSWERS: *(1) c-Adam and Eve, (2) b-olive, (3) c-Temple, (4) e-all of the above, (5) a-Jerusalem, (6) c-Isaiah, (7) b-wither, (8) c-Nebuchadnezzar, (9) b-summer is near, (10) a-Tree of Life*

SCORING: 10 correct—You are ready for a perfect "fall"; 9 correct—You have "raked" in a fairly high score; 8 correct—It's going to be an "average" year for you; 7 or less—Make like a tree and leave this quiz!

Lions and Lambs in the Bible

(An old saying tells us that the month of March comes in either like a lion or a lamb and goes out in just the opposite way. These two animals are also found frequently in the pages of the Bible. Select the correct response concerning the Biblical use of lions and lambs. If you need help with the questions, consider the Biblical reference. If the verse would give away the answer only the passage is giving and not the name of the book.)

1. Lions and lambs were both created on the sixth day of creation (Genesis 1:24) (a) True, (b) False.
2. How many sheep were taken with Noah on the ark (Genesis 7:2)? (a) One, (b) Two, (c) Seven, (d) Fourteen.
3. How many lions were taken with Noah on the ark (Genesis 6:19)? (a) One, (b) Two, (c) Seven, (d) Fourteen.
4. The following Old Testament character became wealthy through the ingenious breeding of lambs (Genesis 30:37-43): (a) Abraham, (b) Isaac, (c) Jacob, (d) Joseph, (e) Reuben.
5. In a final blessing Jacob calls the following of his sons a "lion" (Genesis 49:9) (a) Joseph, (b) Judah, (c) Benjamin, (c) Reuben.
6. On the Day of Atonement the priests in the Bible sacrificed (Leviticus 16:11-16) (a) lambs, (b) goats, (c) bulls, (d) grain, (e) b and c, (f) a and d.
7. The animal sent into the wilderness to "carry away" the people's sins (Leviticus 16:8) was a (a) lion, (b) lamb, (c) scapegoat, (d) bull.
8. According to a riddle told by Samson in the book of Judges the carcass of a lion produced (Judges 14:8) (a) meat, (b) milk, (c) blood, (d) manna, (e) honey.
9. This person killed a lion when he was a boy (I Samuel 17:36): (a) Nathan, (b) David, (c) Samson, (d) Joseph, (e) Jacob.

10. The prophet Nathan charged this man with adultery by telling a story with a lamb (II Samuel 12:1-10) (a) Ahab, (b) Saul, (c) David, (d) Solomon.

11. In the 23rd Psalm the word "lamb" is never mentioned (Psalm 23): (a) True, (b) False.

12. Under Jeroboam's reign in the Old Testament the following man was killed by a lion as God's punishment (I Kings 13:23-25): (a) a prophet, (b) a priest, (c) the king, (d) the queen.

13. Isaiah 53 describes the Messiah as a (a) Lion, (b) Lamb.

14. This prophet tells of a four-headed creature with one face like a lion (1:10): (a) Jeremiah, (b) Isaiah, (c) Zechariah, (d) Ezekiel.

15. This man was thrown into a den of lions, according to the Bible (6:16): (a) Jesus, (b) Daniel, (c) David, (d) Samson.

16. In referring to Jesus the man who said, "Behold the lamb of God which taketh away the sins of the world" was (John 1:29) (a) Peter, (b) Andrew, (c) John, (d) James, (e) Nathaniel.

17. In the New Testament this person told a parable about one lost sheep (Luke 15:1-7) (a) Jesus, (b) Paul, (c) Peter, (d) John.

18. In the following New Testament letter the Apostle Paul says he was delivered from the "lion's mouth" (4:17): (a) Romans, (b) Philippians, (c) Timothy, (d) Philemon.

19. The following New Testament writer calls Satan a lion (5:8): (a) Paul, (b) Luke, (c) Peter, (d) John.

20. The book of Revelation continually refers to Jesus as a (chapters 5-7) (a) lion, (b) lamb.

ANSWERS: (1) a, (2) d, (3) b, (4) c, (5) b, (6) e, (7) c, (8) e, (9) b, (10) c, (11) a, (12) a, (13) b, (14) d, (15) b, (16) c, (17) a, (18) c, (19) c, (20) b

SCORING: 20-19 correct – Like a bold lion, you knew the answers, 18-17 correct – You know the lamb of God who takes away the sin of the world, 16-15 – You march to a different drummer, 14-13 – No "lion" ("Know lion"); you could have done better!

Lost People in the Bible

(Getting lost is no fun. For children, it can be frightening. For adults, it can be embarrassing. Also, some of us would not admit being lost, even when it is obvious. Being "lost" from God is especially troubling. See if you can determine who is "lost" from the pages of the Bible. Check the Bible reference if you need help.)

1. "I wasn't really lost because my mother purposely put me in a stream, but, still, I was found by Pharaoh's daughter. Who am I?" *(Exodus 2:1-10)*
2. "I got 'lost' but my parents found me in the temple, listening to and teaching the great men of God in my Father's house. Who am I?" *(Luke 2:41-52)*
3. "Beyond my mention as having been elected a new apostle to replace Judas, all other details of my life are 'lost.' Who am I?" *(Acts 1:23-26)*
4. "When my father greeted me after my long absence he explained to my unforgiving brother (who may have also been 'lost'), that I was 'lost but now found.' Who am I?" *(Luke 15:11-32)*
5. "I wrote one of the books of the New Testament, but my name has been lost as author. What book did I write?" *(19ᵗʰ New Testament book)*
6. "Because my half-brother was the legal heir to my father's line and promise and I was the son of a slave woman I had to move away from my mother and become 'lost.' Who am I?" *(Genesis 21:8-21)*
7. "I 'lost' my life in the Bible because of my brother's lack of true worship and because of his anger when God was displeased with his offering. Who am I?" *(Genesis 4:1-12)*
8. "I 'lost' my rightful inheritance by selling it for a 'mess of pottage' or red stew. Who am I?" *(Genesis 25:27-34)*

9. "I 'lost' favor with the people in a showdown on Mt. Carmel because the true God showed that He was more powerful than I was. Who am I?" *(I Kings 18:25-40)*

10. "The book of God's law was 'lost' prior to my reign as king but I helped 'rediscover' it. Who am I?" *(II Kings 22:1-13)*

11. "I promised to help Joseph who had interpreted my dreams in prison but this idea was 'lost' for a couple of years when my dreams came true. Later I remembered him when Pharaoh needed help with his dreams. Who am I?" *(Genesis 41:9-14)*

12. "I 'lost' my inheritance rights when my husband and my sons died because my sons were married to pagan girls. Later I talked my faithful daughter-in-law into marrying one of the people of Israel and they had a child who became an ancestor of David, the greatest king of Israel. Who am I?" *(Ruth 1:3-5, 4:13-16)*

13. "I felt that I was 'lost' when I witnessed a vision of the Lord God in His temple, but He showed me that He had work for me to do and I was happy to respond. I am the first 'major' prophet and quoted in the New Testament more than any other prophet. Who am I?" *(6:5)*

14. "I was one of 100 animals which were 'lost' in a parable spoken by Jesus. What am I?" *(Luke 15:1-7)*

15. "In an attempt to win away one of God's most faithful servants I found myself working in vain. I tried everything, from destroying his family and his economic security to harming his friendships. However, I still 'lost' the battle and he remained steadfast in his faith and to his God. Who am I?" *(Job 1-2, 42)*

ANSWERS: (1) Moses, (2) Jesus, (3) Matthias, (4) Prodigal Son or "Lost Son," (5) Hebrews, (6) Ishmael, (7) Abel, (8) Esau, (9) Baal, (10) Josiah, (11) Cupbearer or Butler, (12) Naomi, (13) Isaiah, (14) Sheep, (15) Devil (Satan).

SCORING: 15 correct: You did not get lost in this quiz; 14 or 13 correct: People who didn't know as many answers as you are "lost"; 12 or 11 correct: I'm at a loss to appreciate how well you've done; 10 or fewer correct: Get a little more lost in your study of the Word.

March Madness in the Bible

(March is the month for basketball's "March Madness." Basketball isn't mentioned in the Bible, though the Apostle Paul does write about sports and games. It might not be "politically correct" to use the phrase "madness" to describe people's lives but we offer this "March Madness" quiz on individuals in the Bible who dealt with extreme physical and emotional challenges. Check the Biblical reference if you need help.)

1. God warns His people about disobedience and the threat of captivity and declares *(Deuteronomy 28:34)* (a) the sights they see would drive them mad, (b) their leaders would go insane, (c) the women would remain normal but the men would be insane, (d) none of the above, (e) all of the above.

2. This man pretended to be insane to confuse Achish, king of Gath, who said, "Am I so short of madmen that you have to bring this fellow here?" *(I Samuel 21:12-15)*: (a) Abraham, (b) Moses, (c) Joseph, (d) David, (e) Jonah.

3. Solomon, the author of Ecclesiastes, says that he applied himself to understanding wisdom and folly and *(Ecclesiastes 1:18, 2:12)* (a) insanity, (b) madness, (c) grumpiness, (d) psychology.

4. This nation with high natural stone walls laughed at Israel's plight and God said, "You too, O Madmen, will be silenced" *(Jeremiah 48:2)*: (a) Cana, (b) Babylon, (c) Moab, (d) Philistia.

5. In an oracle and vision on the final destruction of Jerusalem *(Zechariah 12:3-4)* Zechariah sees a vision of (a) people injuring themselves, (b) a horse with panic, (c) horses that are blinded, (d) riders with madness, (e) all of the above.

6. King Nebuchadnezzar of Babylon was warned by God about impending insanity because of his wickedness and

the following happened to him *(Daniel 4:24-34):* (a) he lived with wild animals, (b) he ate grass like cattle, (c) his hair grew like the feathers of an eagle, (d) his nails grew like the claws of a bird, (e) all of the above.

7. This group tried to take charge of Jesus because they said, "He is out of His mind" *(Mark 3:21):* (a) His family, (b) the Pharisees, (c) the Sadducees, (d) the Levites, (e) the Roman Soldiers.

8. In the area of the Gerasenes Jesus healed a man *(Mark 5:1-9)* (a) who had an evil spirit, (b) who lived in the tombs, (c) who was able to tear chains apart, (d) who cut himself with stones, (e) who called himself Legion, (f) all of the above.

9. When Paul talked to this leader, the man said that Paul was being driven insane by his great learning *(Acts 26:24):* (a) Felix, (b) Agrippa, (c) Festus, (d) Bernice, (e) none of the above.

10. This man writes, "The evil I do not want to do—this I keep on doing" *(Romans 7:19).* What is his name? (a) Peter, (b) John, (c) Barnabas, (d) Paul, (e) none of the above.

11. As Paul writes to the Corinthians he says *(II Corinthians 11:21-25)* (a) he was not one of Abraham's descendants, (b) he was out of his mind to talk like this, (c) he had never been in prison, (d) he had never been flogged, (e) all of the above, (f) none of the above.

12. Peter describes this evil Old Testament prophet who was confronted by a talking donkey and speaks about his madness *(II Peter 2:1-16):* (a) Gehazi, (b) Balaam, (c) Eli, (d) none of the above.

ANSWERS: *(1) a/the sights they see would drive them mad, (2) d/David, (3) b/madness, (4) c/Moab, (5) e/all of the above, (6) e/all of the above, (7)* *a/His family, (8) f/all of the above, (9) c/Festus, (10) d/Paul, (11) b/he was out of his mind to talk like this, (12) b/Balaam>*

SCORING: 12 correct – You win the tournament!; 11 or 10 correct – You don't need a "bye", 9 correct – "March" up to the prize table; 8 or less correct – Don't get mad; you could do better.

Memorials in the Bible

(Memorial Day is now a federal holiday celebrated the last Monday of May. The observance dates back to a time after the Civil War when those who served or gave their lives in military service. In today's world it is also a time to remember loved ones who have died. Memorials are physical symbols of remembrance or honor or death and are often created to remember individuals, battles or events. See if you can determine the Biblical "memorials" being described in the clues given. If you need help, check the Bible reference.)

1. When God displaced His first created beings from the Garden of Eden and His presence I was sent to guard and protect them from re-entering and eating from the Tree of Life. My "memorial" was a flaming sword that I held. (Genesis 3:24) Who am I? (a) Cherubim, (b) seraphim, (c) Michael, (d) Gabriel.

2. We built a tower not so much as a memorial but as a symbol of our dominance in the world. However, God was not pleased with our structure and ended up confusing the builders. (Genesis 11:1-9) What was this "memorial" called? (a) Shinar, (b) Babel, (c) Enoch, (d) Arpachshad.

3. I was not really a memorial but my death and what I became symbolized the temptation to look back at things in life rather than to look to God and I became a symbol and memorial of disobedience. My name is not mentioned but my husband and I lived in the evil cities of Sodom and Gomorrah. What was his name? (Genesis 19:23-26) (a) Cain, (b) Tubal-Cain, (c) Lot, (d) Ur, (e) Haran.

4. My name is Abraham and when my wife Sarah died I refused to let the Hittites donate her grave to me. Instead, I willingly paid for it, confident that someday this land would be for my descendants, as God had promised. What was the name of the place where I buried Sarah?

(Genesis 23:1-16) (a) Cave of Machpelah, (b) Ur of the Chaldees, (c) Cave of the Medes and Persians, (d) The Wadi in the Negev.

5. I set up a pillar of stone after leaving Paddan-aram and hearing God again promise to me that he would give to me and my offspring the land before me. I poured a drink offering and oil on this pillar and I called it "Bethel." Who am I? (Genesis 35:9-15) (a) Abraham, (b) Isaac, (c) Jacob, (d) Joseph.

6. My name is Moses and at God's command I constructed a snake on a pole to symbolize healing and this was a reminder of the coming cross and death of Jesus. Unfortunately, some of God's people ended up worshiping this "memorial" snake on a pole and even burned incense to it. What was the name of this "snake"? (Numbers 21:8-9, II Kings 18:4, John 3:14-15) (a) Bethel, (b) Ebenezer, (c) Nehushtan, (d) Negev

7. When I led God's people and tribes into the Promised Land we crossed the Jordan River and God told us to establish a special "Memorial Forever" to commemorate this event. What was this "memorial"? (Joshua 4:4-7) (a) Twelve stones, (b) Ark of the Covenant, (c) Ebenezer, (d) Job's Daughters.

8. My name is Samuel and I authorized a memorial stone to be set up to commemorate God's victory in a great battle against the Philistines when they were totally defeated and the Ark of the Covenant was recaptured. (I Samuel 7:7-12, 4:10). What was the named of this rock memorial? (a) Petras, (b) Ebenezer, (c) Jonah's Rock, (d) Pisgah.

9. Though I did not build the Temple I got things ready for the building of the Temple and encouraged people to make freewill offerings for this work to get done and the gifts flowed in freely. Who am I? (I Chronicles 29) (a) Solomon, (b) Abiathar, (c) Asaph, (d) David, (e) Hiram.

10. My name is Esther and I became Queen of Persia but in order to protect my people I had to put my life on the

line and plead to the King for their deliverance from the evil plot of a man named Haman. Because of this deliverance a memorial celebration was begun. What was this celebration called? (Esther 9:26-32) (a) Purim, (b) Passover, (c) Pentecost, (d) Hanukkah.

11. My name is Lemuel and in my writings in the book of Proverbs compiled by Solomon I said that a woman of noble character should receive something for her special role and work in life, a type of "memorial." What did I say that she should receive? (Proverbs 31:10-31) (a) Heaven, (b) Praise, (c) a Statue, (d) a Church building.

12. My name is Jesus and it wasn't a memorial but a woman at Simon the Leper's house anointed me with expensive ointment and I said that this would always be remembered "in memory of her." (Matthew 26:6-13). In what city did this take place? (a) Bethlehem, (b) Jerusalem, (c) Bethany, (c) Nazareth, (d) Emmaus.

13. Though it wasn't exactly a memorial, this field was purchased with 30 pieces of silver because of the death of a certain person. Whose death was this? (Matthew 27:3-10). (a) Judas Iscariot, (b) Jesus Christ, (c) James the Apostle, (d) Lazarus.

14. My name is Paul and when I was in this city I saw this "altar" which was something like a "memorial" to an unknown "god." I used this opportunity to talk about the "real" God and Savior who is Jesus. What city was I in? (Acts 17:22-28). (a) Rome, (b) Lystra, (c) Ephesus, (d) Athens.

15. My name is John and I received God's messages to the seven churches of the book of Revelation. One of the churches received word that those who conquered would receive a white stone with their name on it, a type of "memorial." Which church was being addressed? (Revelation 2:12-17) (a) Laodicea, (b) Smyrna, (c) Pergamum, (d) Philadelphia, (e) All of the above, (f) None of the above.

ANSWERS: *(1) a/Cherubim, (2) b/Babel, (3) c/Lot, (4) a/Cave of Machpelah, (5) c/Jacob, (6) c/Nehushtan, (7) a/Twelve Stones, (8) b/ Ebenezer, (9) d/David, (10) a/Purim, (11) b/Praise, (12) c/Bethany, (13) a/Judas Iscariot, (14) d/Athens, (15) c/Pergamum.*

SCORING: 15 correct – Your "memory" is great; 14 or 13 correct – You could receive a memorial plaque!; 12 or 11 correct – You see many "signs" of God's presence, 10 or fewer correct – Look around to see more of God's mighty acts.

Ministry in the Book of Acts

(Preparing people for the ministry is part of a Biblical tradition and pastors, ministers, teachers, deacons and missionaries are mentioned in the Bible in many places. See if you can determine the men and women being described in "ministry" in the Early Church in the book of Acts with the clues given. If you need help, you may wish to check the Bible passage given.)

1. Not everything in the Early Church was positive. We responded to the Gospel message by making large monetary gifts based on a piece of property. We lied about his, however, and both of us ended up losing our lives. Do you know our names? (Acts 5:1-11) (a) Priscilla and Aquila, (b) Ahab and Jezebel, (c) Ananias and Sapphira, (d) Philippi jailer and his wife.

2. When the disciples were struggling with having enough people to "serve" they decided to choose seven people to work with them. I was one of these seven and I ended up as one of the first people to give their life for the cause of Christ. What is my name? (Acts 6:3-6, 7:54-60) (a) Paul, (b) Silas, (c) John Mark, (d) Stephen.

3. I came to believe in Jesus through the ministry of Philip but my faith was questionable because when I saw Peter and John baptize people with the Holy Spirit I tried to buy this power. Who am I? (Acts 8:9-24) (a) Simon the Magician, (b) Felix the governor, (c) Andrew the Eunuch, (d) Cornelius from Caesarea.

4. I was an enemy of Christian people and even had them arrested until Jesus appeared to me on the Damascus road. Who am I? (Acts 9:1-9) (a) Barnabas, (b) John Mark, (c) Silas, (d) Saul, (e) none of the above.

5. My ministry to the Paul was to pray over him and baptize him. I was reluctant to do this but God commanded me

to complete the task. What's my name? (Acts 9:10-18) (a) Barnabas, (b) Ananias, (c) John Mark, (d) Silas.

6. My work of ministry was in doing acts of charity, including making garments. When I became ill and died I was healed through the power of God with Simon Peter praying over me. (Acts 9:36-41) What's my name? (a) Tabitha, (b) Dorcas, (c) Mary, (d) "a" and "b", (e) none of the above.

7. I am not listed as a pastor or minister but my ministry included ministry of prayer and giving and in answer to prayer, Simon Peter was sent by God to minister in Caesarea. Who am I? (Acts 10:1-2, 30-31) (a) Aeneas, (b) Saul, (c) Cornelius, (d) Simon Magnus.

8. I am called an apostle but I was not one of the original disciples. Part of my work was serving as a missionary who first defended Saul and who encouraged the church to accept him and his work. Who am I? (Acts 11:22-26. (a) Paul, (b) Barnabas, (c) Silas, (d) John Mark.

9. There are several people in the Bible with my name including one of the disciples. He was killed, however, and I ended up as the president or leader of the church. Do you know my name? (Acts 15:12-21) (a) James, (b) John, (c) Andrew, (d) Peter.

10. I am mentioned several times in the New Testament. I was a protégé of the Apostle Paul and served as a minister. My father was Greek and my mother was Jewish. The implication of the Bible is that I was nervous and timid but I was taught well by my mother and grandmother. Who am I? (Acts 16:1-3) (a) John Mark, (b) Titus, (c) Timothy, (d) Luke.

11. Some people suggest that I wrote the book of Hebrews but there is nothing in the Bible about this. I was an eloquent speaker but I needed to be taught by Priscilla and Aquila and others. Give my name. (Acts 18:24-28) (a) Paul, (b) Barnabas, (c) Philemon (d) Titus, (e) Apollos.

12. I was young but I was busy listening to Paul preach and growing in my faith. Unfortunately, I fell asleep during one of his sermons and fell three stories to my death but, praise God, Paul prayed over me and I was healed. Do you know my name? (Acts 20:7-12) (a) Eutychus, (b) Apollos, (c) Titus, (d) Philemon,

ANSWERS: *(1) c-Ananias and Sapphira, (2) d-Stephen, (3) a-Simon the Magician, (4) d-Saul, (5) b-Ananias, (6) d-"a" and "b", (7) c-Cornelius, (8) b-Barnabas, (9) a-James, (10) c-Timothy, (11) e-Apollos, (12) a-Eutychus.*

SCORING: 12 Correct-You don't just "act" like you know it; you know it, 11 Correct-You know the Early Church well, 10 Correct-Keep digging in the word and you will be blessed, 9 or fewer correct-Turn back to the book of Acts for more help.

Mothers in the Bible (with multiple clues)

(There are many famous mothers in the Bible. How many clues will it take for you to guess the mother being described? Three clues are given, plus the Bible reference as a fourth and final "clue." In some cases the mother's name is not given in the Bible so these mothers would need to be identified with their husband's name.)

1. Who am I?
   - I was called "mother of all living."
   - My first son was murdered.
   - My third son was named "Seth."
   - Biblical "clue": Genesis 3:20

2. Who am I?
   - My original name suggested being childless or barren.
   - I gave my maidservant to my husband to be a surrogate mother.
   - I laughed in my old age when told I would be a mother.
   - Biblical "clue": Genesis 17:15

3. Who am I?
   - My husband's name was Hosea.
   - I ran away from my spouse and became a harlot.
   - I had three children with very long names.
   - Biblical "clue": Hosea 1:2-3

4. Who am I?
   - Both my husband and I were from the tribe of Judah.
   - An angel told me that I would be a mother.
   - I saw my oldest son die.
   - Biblical "clue": Luke 1:34-38

5. Who am I?
    - I had three sons who survived a flood.
    - I helped my husband build a boat far from water.
    - My name is not given in the Bible.
    - Biblical "clue": Genesis 7:7

6. Who am I?
    - My sister married my husband first.
    - I was mother to two sons named Benjamin and Joseph.
    - I died in childbirth.
    - Biblical "clue": Genesis 35:16-18

7. Who am I?
    - I was mother of twin boys.
    - I became the fiancé of Isaac in answer to the prayer of Abraham's servant.
    - I helped my younger son trick his father and my husband.
    - Biblical "clue": Genesis 25:24-26

8. Who am I?
    - I was praised by Paul for my Christian walk.
    - My son Timothy was raised in the faith.
    - My mother, Lois, was also a devout Christian as we raised my son.
    - Biblical "clue": II Timothy 1:5

9. Who am I?
    - My daughter was married to a famous fisherman.
    - I lived in Capernaum.
    - I was healed by Jesus in a miracle.
    - Biblical "clue": Matthew 8:14-15

10. Who am I?
    - My first husband died away from his ancestral home.
    - I cared deeply for my mother-in-law.

- I was an ancestor of King David.
- Biblical "clue": Ruth 4:13-17

11. Who am I?
- I prayed fervently about being childless.
- I promised that my firstborn son would live in the temple.
- I was the mother of Samuel.
- Biblical "clue": I Samuel 1:19-20

12. Who am I?
- I lost ten children in a terrible accident.
- When we suffered our terrible losses I told my husband to curse God and die.
- I was blessed with more children after my husband's time of testing was over.
- Biblical "clue": Job 2:9-10

13. Who am I?
- My husband was struck speechless for not believing God's promise.
- I was cousin to the mother of Jesus.
- I was mother to the last great prophet.
- Biblical "clue": Luke 1:57-60

14. Who am I?
- I made a bold request to Jesus concerning my sons.
- I was mother to the two closest disciples of Jesus.
- My name means "peace."
- Biblical "clue": Matthew 27:56, Mark 15:40

15. Who am I?
- I hid my son in a little boat.
- I ended up raising my own son at the request of Pharaoh's daughter.
- My other two children were named Aaron and Miriam.
- Biblical "clue": Exodus 2:1-10, Exodus 6:20

16. Who am I?
- My first husband was named Uriah.
- I first got involved with my future husband in an adulterous union.
- I was the mother of Solomon.
- Biblical "clue": II Samuel 12:15, 24-25

17. Who am I?
- I mothered six children.
- My husband's name was Jacob.
- I was not loved like my sister was.
- Biblical "clue": Genesis 29:16-30, Genesis 35:23

18. Who am I?
- My husband's name was Phinehas.
- My son's name was Ichabod which means "the glory has departed."
- My son was born on the day that my father in law died and the ark of the covenant was captured. Though my name is not give my father in law's name is.
- Biblical "clue": I Samuel 4:17-22

19. Who am I?
- I was a surrogate mother for Sarai.
- I was driven away from the father of my child because of jealousy.
- My child's name was Ishmael.
- Biblical "clue": Genesis 16:1-12

20. Who am I?
- I was childless for many years until I saw an angel of the Lord in the field.
- My son, Samson, was to be raised following a special Nazarite vow.

- Though my name is not given you can identify me through my husband's name.
- Biblical "clue": Judges 13:2-5, Judges 13:24-25

ANSWERS: (1) Eve, (2) Sarai or Sarah, (3) Gomer, (4) Mary, (5) Noah's wife, (6) Rachel, (7) Rebekah, (8) Eunice, (9) Peter's mother in law, (10) Ruth, (11) Hannah, (12) Job's wife, (13) Elizabeth, (14) Salome, (15) Jocebed, (16) Bathsheba, (17) Leah, (18) Eli's daughter in law, (19) Hagar, (20) Manoah.

SCORING: 20 or 19 Correct: You have done very well in this "mother" of all quizzes!; 17 or 18 Correct: You have spent time with these mothers; 15 or 16 Correct: Check with Mom; Less than 15 Correct: Some motherly advice: "Study the Bible even more!"

New in the Old Testament

(New things always seem to be happening, whether it be a New Year, a new school year, a new job, or a new child. What does the Old Testament say about "new"? See if you can determine the answers to "New in the Bible" without checking the Biblical reference.)

1. I was the first "newborn" in the Bible—in fact I was the first person "born" in the Bible. Who am I? (Genesis 3:1-2) (a) Abel, (b) Cain, (c) Seth, (d) Abraham, (e) None of the above.

2. I was called a new "king" in Egypt who began to oppress God's people many years after the death of Joseph and his family. By what other name am I called? (Exodus 1:8) (a) Pharaoh, (b) Solomon, (c) Nebuchadnezzar, (d) Cyrus, (e) None of the above.

3. This "rule of law" about something new would exempt a person from military service. What was this law? (Deuteronomy 24:5) (a) Person with new property, (b) Person with a new vow to serve in the Temple, (c) Person with a new wife, (d) Person with a new ox, (e) None of the above.

4. I was bound with two new ropes because this was supposed to keep me from attacking my captors. By the way, it didn't work. Who am I? (Judges 15:13) (a) David, (b) Gideon, (c) Solomon, (d) Jeremiah, (e) Samson.

5. This was returned to Israel after being captive for more than half a year. Several "new" things were needed for its return. What was it? (I Samuel 6:7-10) (a) Ark of the Covenant, (b) Temple brass, (c) Urim and Thummin, (d) Brass serpent on a pole, (e) None of the above.

6. This new place was built during the reign of Solomon and was dedicated with great pomp. (I Kings 6:37-38) What

was it? (a) Ark of the Covenant, (b) Solomon's palace, (c) The Temple, (d) City of Bethel, (e) None of the above.

7. I wrote that there was "nothing new under the sun." (Ecclesiastes 1:9-10) (a) Solomon, (b) Koheleth, (c) the Preacher, (d) the Teacher, (e) All of the above.

8. I, Isaiah, wrote about this person and talked about singing a "new song" to Him. Who am I talking about, under the inspiration of God? (Isaiah 42:10ff.) (a) Solomon, (b) Solomon's son, (c) Solomon's grandson, (d) the Servant of the Lord.

9. This was the place where I, Jeremiah, sat during some of my prophetic preaching and teaching. What place was this? (Jeremiah 26:10, 36:10). (a) the new Temple, (b) the new Ark container, (c) the new King's palace, (d) the new gate at the Temple, (e) the new pulpit.

10. In my prophecy in the book of Ezekiel I talked about many new things. One of the key things that God told me His people would receive was this. (Ezekiel 36:26) (a) new Temple, (b) new Ark, (c) new heart, (d) new feet.

ANSWERS: *(1) b/Cain; (2) a/Pharaoh; (3) c/person with a new wife; (4) e/Samson; (5) a/Ark of the Covenant; (6) c/the Temple; (7) e/all of the above—all are names for Solomon; (8) d/the servant of the Lord; (9) d/the new gate at the Temple; (10) c/new heart.*

SCORING: 10 correct – This quiz wasn't new to you; 9 correct – You have a good handle on new things; 8 – some things are old and new; 7 or less – take a new look at the Old Testament.

New Year in the Bible

(Each January 1 we begin a New Year. What does the Bible say about the "new year"? Try this brief Bible quiz to test your knowledge. See if you can determine the answers to "New Year in the Bible" without checking the Biblical reference.)

1. This man celebrated New Year's Day in his own life (the first day of his 601st year) by celebrating the end of rain and the flood (Genesis 8:13). His name was (a) Abraham, (b) Isaac, (c) Jacob, (d) Noah.

2. In the Old Testament this festival was considered to be the first month of the year for God's people and the tenth day (Exodus 12:1-2). This festival was (a) the Passover (b) the Feast of Unleavened Bread, (c) the time of the Exodus, (d) all of the above, (e) none of the above.

3. After wandering around in the wilderness for a year (but led by God) what did His people do on the first day of the second year (Exodus 40:17)? (a) Built a Golden Calf, (b) Built a Temple, (c) Built and dedicated the Tabernacle, (d) Entered the Promised Land.

4. The fiftieth year (Leviticus 25:8-12) was observed after seven Sabbaths of years (seven times seven) and this year for God's people was to be known as the year of (a) Atonement, (b) Jubilee, (c) Pentecost, (d) Ingathering.

5. This man cut his hair once a year (II Samuel 14:26) and its weight was some 200 shekels. His name was (a) David, (b) Solomon, (c) Absalom, (d) Samson.

6. Jesus talked about the "year of the Lord's favor" (Luke 4:19) when He preached a sermon in (a) Nazareth, (b) Bethlehem, (c) Jerusalem, (d) Capernaum.

7. During the time of Jesus each year in Jerusalem a new high priest was named and during the time when Jesus

raised Lazarus (John 11:40) from the dead this priest was named (a) Annas, (b) Herod, (c) Pilate, (d) Caiaphas.

8. Paul and Barnabas stayed a whole year at this church where the people were first called Christians (Acts 11:26): (a) Jerusalem, (b) Bethlehem, (c) Antioch, (d) Rome

9. Paul was concerned about the Galatian Christians *(Galatians 4:10)* because of their focus on (a) days, (b) months, (c) seasons, (d) years, (e) all of the above.

10. The writer to the Hebrews (Hebrews 10:1-18) talks about this special day once a year when the priest who make a sacrifice which was fulfilled in the sacrifice of Jesus. Name this day: (a) Day of Atonement, (b) Passover, (c) Pentecost, (d) Feast of Booths.

ANSWERS: *(1) d-Noah; (2) d-all of the above; (3) c-Built and dedicated the Tabernacle, (4) b-Jubilee; (5) c-Absalom; (6) a-Nazareth; (7) d-Caiaphas; (8) c-Antioch; (9) e-all of the above; (10) a-Day of Atonement*

SCORING: 10 correct – This quiz wasn't new to you; 9 correct – You have a good handle on new things; 8 correct – Are you ready for the New Year?

Numbers in the Bible

(The Bible is filled with numbers and many of them have special meaning. Learn about numbers as you take this quiz based on numbers in the Bible. If you need help, check your Bible, your concordance or the reference given.)

1. The number of days on which rain poured on the earth during the flood *(Genesis 7:12)*.
2. The number written on the foreheads of unbelievers in Revelation *(Revelation 13:17-18)*.
3. The actual number of "apostles" in the New Testament (according to Paul) *(I Corinthians 15:9)*.
4. The number of days after Christ's resurrection before the coming of the Holy Spirit *(Acts 2:1)*
5. The number of days, not counting the day of rest, that it took God to create the universe *(Genesis 2:2)*.
6. The number of psalms in the Bible.
7. The approximate age of Jesus at the beginning of His ministry *(according to tradition)*.
8. The age of the longest living individual in the Bible, Methuselah *(Genesis 5:27)*.
9. The number of persons in the Trinity.
10. The number of sons that Jacob had *(Genesis 46:8-27)*.
11. The number of "testaments" in the Bible.
12. The number of people saved at the time of the flood *(Genesis 8:15, 9:18)*.
13. The number of commandments *(Exodus 20)*.
14. The number of New Testament Gospel writers.
15. The number of New Testament books written by Mark.
16. The symbolic number of those who will be saved in the book of Revelation *(Revelation 14:1)*.
17. The number of books in the Old Testament *(King James Bible)*.
18. The number of books in the New Testament.

19. The age of Noah at the time of the flood *(Genesis 9:28-29)*.
20. The number of books of Moses in the Old Testament.
21. The number of "men" fed by Jesus in the first miracle with fish and bread *(John 6:10)*.
22. The number of sheep left by the shepherd in search for a lost one *(Matthew 18:12)*
23. The number of lepers who did not thank Jesus for healing *(Luke 17:16-17)*.
24. The number of "books" in the Bible *(King James Bible)*.
25. The number of years before a Jubilee celebration in the Old Testament *(Leviticus 25:11)*.

ANSWERS*: (1) forty, (2) six hundred sixty six, (3) thirteen, (4) fifty, (5) six, (6) one hundred fifty, (7) thirty, (8) nine hundred sixty nine, (9) three, (10) twelve, (11) two, (12) eight, (13) ten, (14) four, (15) one, (16) one hundred forty-four thousand, (17) thirty nine, (18) twenty-seven, (19) five hundred, (20) five, (21) five thousand, (22) ninety-nine, (23) nine, (24) sixty-six, (25) fifty.*

SCORING: 25 correct: You've score 100 per cent; 24 correct: Only off by one number; 23 or 22 correct: Keep counting!; 21 or 20 correct: Your number's not up!; Less than 20 correct: Try to figure things out.

Oil in the Bible

(Oil is on the minds of many people as we consider conversation, global needs, and the dangers of oil spills. Does the Bible talk about oil? It doesn't talk about oil spills but there are many references to oil in the Bible. See if you can determine the answers to "Oil in the Bible" without checking the Biblical reference.)

1. After I had a dream about a ladder or stairway to heaven I set up an altar the next morning and poured oil on top of it. *(Genesis 28:18)* Who am I? (a) Abraham, (b) Isaac, (c) Jacob, (d) David, (e) Solomon.

2. My name is Moses and I was instructed by God to anoint this man and his sons with special anointing oil so that they could be consecrated as priests. What was the name of the man I anointed? *(Exodus 29:6-7)* (a) Melchizedek, (b) Abiathar, (c) Solomon, (d) Aaron, (e) None of the above.

3. We priests were asked to mix the grain offering with oil for the following purpose *(Leviticus 6:21)* (a) to cover sins, (b) for a pleasing aroma for the Lord, (c) for bread for the priests, (d) to feed to the livestock, (e) none of the above.

4. As I blessed the various tribes of Israel before they entered the Promised Land I said that Asher should dip his foot in oil. Maybe his descendants would end up in the Gulf region. *(Deuteronomy 33:1, 24)*. Who am I? (a) Moses, (b) Abraham, (c) Isaac, (d) Jacob, (e) none of the above.

5. I, Samuel, anointed this man with oil as the first king of Israel and referred to this man as a prince who would rule over Israel and save them from their enemies. Read my statement carefully to be sure you have the right man. *(I Samuel 10:1)* (a) David, (b) Solomon, (c) Saul, (d) Absalom, (e) none of the above.

6. I was anointed with oil a man to be king to succeed a leader with problems but which of the following statements about me are true? *(I Samuel 16)* (a) My name is David, (b) I was the youngest and smallest person in my family, (c) my predecessor was extremely jealous of me, (d) I killed an enemy warrior and was cheered because of it, (e) I played the lyre, (f) all of the above are true.

7. With oil I anointed Solomon to be the successor of the greatest king of Israel during a time of great unrest. What is my name? *(I Kings 1:39)* (a) David, (b) Melchizedek, (c) Abiathar, (d) Zadok, (e) Adonijah.

8. My name is David and in this psalm I speak about the head being "anointed with oil." Who is doing the anointing in this beautiful song *(Psalm 23)?* (a) the mother sheep, (b) the shepherd, (c) the merchant, (d) the farmer, (e) none of the above.

9. I warned "my son" about this person's speech being "smoother than oil." To whom am I referring? *(Proverbs 5:3)* (a) a wily preacher, (b) a forbidden woman, (c) a false "god", (d) none of the above, (e) all of the above.

10. My name is Jesus and I quoted this Scripture from Isaiah as I proclaimed my ministry. How did I describe oil in my presentation *(Isaiah 61:3)*? (a) oil of Moses, (b) oil of Solomon, (c) oil of the olive tree, (d) oil of gladness, (e) oil of peace.

11. In my prophecy I ask if the Lord would be pleased with this *(Micah 6:7)*. (a) ten thousand rivers of oil, (b) an oil anointing horn, (c) oil in your name, (d) oil "washed" hands, (e) oil on your head.

12. My name is Jesus and in a parable that I told I spoke about foolish people not taking extra oil. How many people did not take extra oil? *(Matthew 25:1-3)*. (a) ten, (b) seven, (c) five, (d) three, (e) only one.

13. In a parable that Jesus told I was the hero because in my act of mercy I used oil. *(Luke 10:25-37)* Who am

I? (a) Levite, (b) Priest, (c) Sadducee, (d) Pharisee, (e) Samaritan, (f) lawyer.

14. In my New Testament letter (epistle) I wrote that these people should be anointing people with oil *(James 5:14)*. (a) Pastors, (b) Elders, (c) shepherds, (d) kings, (e) prophets.

ANSWERS: *(1) c/Jacob; (2) d/Aaron; (3) b/for a pleasing aroma for the Lord; (4) a/Moses; (5) c/Saul; (6) f/all of the above, (7) d/Zadok; (8) b/the shepherd; (9) b/a forbidden woman; (10) oil of gladness; (11) a/ten thousand rivers of oil; (12) c/five; (13) e/Samaritan; (14) b/Elders.*

SCORING: 14-13 correct – You know your oil!; 12 correct – Only a few drops of oil would be spilled in your presence; 11-10 correct – Find ways to contain any more wrong answers.

Outdoor Worship in the book of Genesis

(From time to time many churches have an outdoor worship service and once in a while people have an outdoor wedding or other worship opportunities "outdoors." In later books of the Bible we discover that even though God had His people build a tabernacle and a temple, He said that no building or piece of furniture should limit our worship. We can worship God anywhere and everywhere. Check the questions below to determine the type of outdoor worship service being suggested by our earliest ancestors in the book of Genesis. For more help, check the Biblical reference.)

1. We had perfect Communion with God in a beautiful, lush garden. There were no buildings, so our worship was definitely "outdoors." Who are we? *(Genesis 2:15-25)*
2. We two brothers had very different occupations in the Bible but when it came to worship we presented our offerings to God "outdoors." One of us presented the first fruits of our labor while the other gave an offering with little or no thought. One of us was blessed and one of us was filled with anger. Who are we? *(Genesis 4:1-5)*
3. After a devastating flood that destroyed and cleansed the entire earth, I was led to sacrifice some of the very animals that I had saved from the flood in an "outdoor" expression of faith. Who am I? *(Genesis 8:20)*
4. We lived in Shinar and we were building something but it wasn't really for worship and, apparently, we were not worshiping "outdoors." We probably weren't thinking about worship but were making a name for ourselves. What was the name of the building that we made? *(Genesis 11:3-4)*
5. When God called me to leave my country and travel I did what He told me to do and ended up living in a tent near Bethel. I didn't build a church building but I built an altar for outdoor worship. Who am I? *(Genesis 12:8-9)*

6. I was a mysterious priest living in "Salem" or ancient Jerusalem. When Lot and his family were rescued, I blessed the man who rescued him in a service that was surely held "outdoors." Who am I? *(Genesis 14:18-20)*.

7. Worship can include laughter but when my husband was "entertaining" strangers and I overheard their suggestion that I would have a child in my old age, my laughter was not related to "outdoor worship." I praise God that my derisive laughter changed to joy when I did indeed bear a child. What is my name? *(Genesis 18:13-15)*

8. My father was severely tested when told by God to sacrifice me on an altar out in the wilderness...definitely "outdoors." I can't say what I thought of God's idea, but I'm thankful that God's angels interrupted this "outdoor worship" service and provided a sacrificial ram rather than me. It was the only time in the Bible that God tested humans in this way. God, of course, tested Himself by sacrificing His own Son, Jesus, to pay for our sins. What is my name? *(Genesis 22:1-19)*

9. I am the same person described in question 5 and I worshipped God in prayer and in an outdoor prayer service, pleading that God would spare two evil cities. What were the names of those cities? *(Genesis 18:16-33)*

10. With a rock for a pillow, I fell asleep during an outdoor "sermon" (not really!) and ended up dreaming of a stairway to heaven. This dreamy worship was God's way of affirming a promise to me and the next morning I built an altar for "outdoor worship." What is my name? *(Genesis 28:10-19)*

11. We never think of wrestling when we think of worship but in a late night prayer time I wrestled with God and with the events that I was facing in the coming days. This "wrestling" was definitely "outdoors." I am the same person mentioned in question 10 but one of the things I was wrestling with was my relationship with my estranged brother. What was his name? *(Genesis 32:22-33:1)*

12. Before my father died in Egypt, he gathered me and all my brothers together to bless us and tell of our future. Though it was not really a worship service, it was part of a tradition in how a patriarch would bless his family. Often this was held outdoors or at the entrance of the family tent. My brothers were somewhat worried about these blessings they might receive because they had sold me into slavery. What is my name? *(All of Genesis chapter 49 and Genesis 50:1)*

ANSWERS: *(1) Adam and Eve, (2) Cain and Abel, (3) Noah, (4) Babel, (5) Abraham, (6) Melchizedek, (7) Sarah, (8) Isaac, (9) Sodom and Gomorrah, (10) Jacob, (11) Esau, (12) Joseph.*

SCORING: 12 Correct: Places do not matter but your score does; 11 Correct: God is with you where ever you go; 10 Correct: Worship God in Spirit and in truth; 9 or fewer Correct: Check out more places to worship.

Places People "Stayed" in the Bible

("Washington slept here" is a well-known phrase. He didn't stay in any Biblical locations but in this quiz with two answers per question, you are asked to supply the names of famous people in the Bible and where they stayed. Use the list below of people/persons and the second list as to where they stayed to complete the quiz. For more help, consult the Bible passage listed.)

Persons:

Noah's family	Jonah	Jesus	Adam/Eve
Elijah	Lot	Joseph	Paul
John	Jeremiah		

Places:

Ark	Fish (Whale)	Zacchaeus	
Widow's	Sodom/Gomorrah	Potiphar	Prison
Patmos	Pit	Edem	

1. Person/People _____ and where they stayed _____. We stayed in a beautiful garden until we didn't obey the rules of the owner. He told us that He was kicking us out "for our own protection." Who are we are where were we staying? (Genesis 2:8, 3:22-24)

2. Person/People _____ and where they stayed _____. We lived in the water for a long period of time during a flood. The place we stayed was large and roomy but we shared it with a lot of animals. Who are we and where did we stay? (Genesis 7:1-2)

3. Person/People _____ and where they stayed _____. When three people visited

my home in the Old Testament. I warned them that they had to stay the night with me because our city was so evil. Who stayed with me and what was the name of the cities? (Genesis 19:1-3)

4. Person/People _____ and where they stayed _____. I was a reluctant guest in this man's house because I had been sold into slavery and now I had to contend with this man's wife. Who am I and at whose house did I stay? (Genesis 39:1-23)

5. Person/People _____ and where they stayed _____. I stayed at the home of someone who took me in, despite the lack of food in her home. It was during a famine, so I provided a way for my hostess to have food. Who am I and at whose house did I stay? (I Kings 17:8-16)

6. Person/People _____ and where they stayed _____. I was a prophet who spent some time in a very undesirable place. I was thrown into this place because I had preached God's Word and had warned the people of God's judgment. Who am I and where was I forced to stay? (Jeremiah 38:1-6)

7. Person/People _____ and where they stayed _____. I stayed in very cramped living quarters for three days while God impressed upon me the need to complete my mission. Finally, God heard my prayer and I was thrown out of my living quarters. Who am I and where did I stay? (Jonah 1:17, 2:10).

8. Person/People _____ and where they stayed _____. I stayed in the house of a short man who climbed a tree in order to get a better glimpse of men. Who am I and at whose house did I stay? (Luke 19:1-10).

9. Person/People _____ and where they stayed _____. I stayed in this kind of dwelling several times during my ministry. On one of these stays I wrote a letter of joy and hope to a congregation

who supported me with their prayers and gifts. Who am I and where was I staying? (Ephesians 3:1, 4:1)

10. Person/People _____ and where they stayed _____. I was the disciple "whom Jesus loved" and very late in my life I stayed on a small island and received a vision of the church's future. Who am I and on what island was I staying? (Revelation 1:9-11)

ANSWERS: *(1) Adam/Eve, Eden; (2) Noah's family, Ark; (3) Lot, Sodom/ Gomorrah; (4) Joseph, Potiphar; (5) Elijah, Widow's home; (6) Jeremiah, Pit; (7) Jonah, Fish (Whale); (8) Jesus, Zacchaeus; (9) Paul, Prison; (10) John, Patmos.*

SCORING: 20 Correct: You know where you are going and where you have been; 19 Correct: I'm sure people would love to stay with you; 18 Correct: Do you think you have the gift of hospitality?; 17 Correct: Clean your house because company might be coming!; 16 or Fewer Correct: Have you been wandering around?

Prayer in the Bible

(Someone has described prayer as "talking with God." We open our hearts to God and He listens and answers. His answers vary—"Yes" or "No" or "Wait." Sometimes God loves us too much to give us what we think we want. There are many prayers in the Bible. See if you can determine the Biblical "prayers" being described in the clues given. If you need help, check the Bible reference.)

1. When God displaced His first created beings from the Garden of Eden and His presence I was sent to guard and protect them from re-entering and eating from the Tree of Life. My "memorial" was a flaming sword that I held. (Genesis 3:24) Who am I? (a) Cherubim, (b) seraphim, (c) Michael, (d) Gabriel.

2. We built a tower not so much as a memorial but as a symbol of our dominance in the world. However, God was not pleased with our structure and ended up confusing the builders. (Genesis 11:1-9) What was this "memorial" called? (a) Shinar, (b) Babel, (c) Enoch, (d) Arpachshad.

3. I was not really a memorial but my death and what I became symbolized the temptation to look back at things in life rather than to look to God and I became a symbol and memorial of disobedience. My name is not mentioned but my husband and I lived in the evil cities of Sodom and Gomorrah. What was his name? (Genesis 19:23-26) (a) Cain, (b) Tubal-Cain, (c) Lot, (d) Ur, (e) Haran.

4. My name is Abraham and when my wife Sarah died I refused to let the Hittites donate her grave to me. Instead, I willingly paid for it, confident that someday this land would be for my descendants, as God had promised. What was the name of the place where I buried Sarah? (Genesis 23:1-16) (a) Cave of Machpelah, (b) Ur of the

Chaldees, (c) Cave of the Medes and Persians, (d) The Wadi in the Negev.

5. I set up a pillar of stone after leaving Paddan-aram and hearing God again promise to me that he would give to me and my offspring the land before me. I poured a drink offering and oil on this pillar and I called it "Bethel." Who am I? (Genesis 35:9-15) (a) Abraham, (b) Isaac, (c) Jacob, (d) Joseph.

6. My name is Moses and at God's command I constructed a snake on a pole to symbolize healing and this was a reminder of the coming cross and death of Jesus. Unfortunately, some of God's people ended up worshiping this "memorial" snake on a pole and even burned incense to it. What was the name of this "snake"? (Numbers 21:8-9, II Kings 18:4, John 3:14-15) (a) Bethel, (b) Ebenezer, (c) Nehushtan, (d) Negev

7. When I led God's people and tribes into the Promised Land we crossed the Jordan River and God told us to establish a special "Memorial Forever" to commemorate this event. What was this "memorial"? (Joshua 4:4-7) (a) Twelve stones, (b) Ark of the Covenant, (c) Ebenezer, (d) Job's Daughters.

8. My name is Samuel and I authorized a memorial stone to be set up to commemorate God's victory in a great battle against the Philistines when they were totally defeated and the Ark of the Covenant was recaptured. (I Samuel 7:7-12, 4:10). What was the named of this rock memorial? (a) Petras, (b) Ebenezer, (c) Jonah's Rock, (d) Pisgah.

9. Though I did not build the Temple I got things ready for the building of the Temple and encouraged people to make freewill offerings for this work to get done and the gifts flowed in freely. Who am I? (I Chronicles 29) (a) Solomon, (b) Abiathar, (c) Asaph, (d) David, (e) Hiram.

10. My name is Esther and I became Queen of Persia but in order to protect my people I had to put my life on the line and plead to the King for their deliverance from

the evil plot of a man named Haman. Because of this deliverance a memorial celebration was begun. What was this celebration called? (Esther 9:26-32) (a) Purim, (b) Passover, (c) Pentecost, (d) Hanukkah.

11. My name is Lemuel and in my writings in the book of Proverbs compiled by Solomon I said that a woman of noble character should receive something for her special role and work in life, a type of "memorial." What did I say that she should receive? (Proverbs 31:10-31) (a) Heaven, (b) Praise, (c) a Statue, (d) a Church building.

12. My name is Jesus and it wasn't a memorial but a woman at Simon the Leper's house anointed me with expensive ointment and I said that this would always be remembered "in memory of her." (Matthew 26:6-13). In what city did this take place? (a) Bethlehem, (b) Jerusalem, (c) Bethany, (c) Nazareth, (d) Emmaus.

13. Though it wasn't exactly a memorial, this field was purchased with 30 pieces of silver because of the death of a certain person. Whose death was this? (Matthew 27:3-10). (a) Judas Iscariot, (b) Jesus Christ, (c) James the Apostle, (d) Lazarus.

14. My name is Paul and when I was in this city I saw this "altar" which was something like a "memorial" to an unknown "god." I used this opportunity to talk about the "real" God and Savior who is Jesus. What city was I in? (Acts 17:22-28). (a) Rome, (b) Lystra, (c) Ephesus, (d) Athens.

15. My name is John and I received God's messages to the seven churches of the book of Revelation. One of the churches received word that those who conquered would receive a white stone with their name on it, a type of "memorial." Which church was being addressed? (Revelation 2:12-17) (a) Laodicea, (b) Smyrna, (c) Pergamum, (d) Philadelphia, (e) All of the above, (f) None of the above.

Pastor Willis Schwichtenberg

ANSWERS: *(1) a/Cherubim, (2) b/Babel, (3) c/Lot, (4) a/Cave of Machpelah, (5) c/Jacob, (6) c/Nehushtan, (7) a/Twelve Stones, (8) b/ Ebenezer, (9) d/David, (10) a/Purim, (11) b/Praise, (12) c/Bethany, (13) a/Judas Iscariot, (14) d/Athens, (15) c/Pergamum.*

SCORING: 15 correct – Your "memory" is great; 14 or 13 correct – You could receive a memorial plaque!; 12 or 11 correct – You see many "signs" of God's presence, 10 or fewer correct – Look around to see more of God's mighty acts.

President's Day in the Bible

(President's Day is celebrated in the month of February. No, presidents are not mentioned in the Bible. However, when we think of the two presidential birthdays that we commemorate in February we especially think of George Washington who is sometimes called the "Father of Our Country." Let's run with that thought and think of fathers and founding fathers in the Bible in this little "presidential" quiz. If you need help, you may wish to check the Bible passage given. If the Bible reference would give away the answer only the verse reference is given.)

1. Just as Eve is known as the "mother of all living" we could refer to this man as the "father of all living" (Genesis 3:20). His name is (a) Adam, (b) Cain, (c) Abel, (d) Seth.
2. This man was called the "father of those who play lyres and pipes" (Genesis 4:21) What was his name? (a) Lyrica, (b) Jubal, (c) Musik, (d) Pippa.
3. Today the Patriarch Abraham is recognized as the "father" of several religions and is often called the "Father of the Jewish Nation." Abraham was also a physical father. Who was his first child? (Genesis 15:16) (a) Isaac, (b) Ishmael, (c) Eleazor, (d) none of the above.
4. God added the word "ham" to this man's name (Genesis 17:5) because (a) his father Noah survived the flood, (b) he could now eat pork, (c) he liked to tell jokes, (d) he would be the father of many nations.
5. This man had twelve sons who were the leaders of the twelve tribes of Israel. His sons were far from perfect but they were the ones whom God chose to eventually populate the Holy Land. Name this Father of the Twelve Tribes. (Genesis 35:22) (a) Abraham, (b) Isaac, (c) Jacob, (d) Joseph.
6. God gave the Law on Mt. Sinai to this man who might be called the "Father of the Law." (Exodus 19:25, 20:1)

What was his name? (a) Joshua, (b) Moses, (c) Jochebed, (d) Zipporah.

7. Since he built the Temple this man could be called the "Father of the Temple." What was his name? (I Kings 6:1-2) (a) David, (b) Jeroboam, (c) Solomon, (d) Absalom.

8. This man could be called the "father of the queen" and his adopted daughter has a Biblical book which bears her name. (Esther 2:15, 22) What was his name? (a) Mordecai, (b) Haman, (c) Bigtha, (d) Xerxes.

9. Many of the Psalms praise God for who He is. One psalm refers to Him with the following title (Psalm 68:5). Give the title. (a) father of the universe, (b) father of the human race, (c) father of the fatherless, (d) all of the above, (e) none of the above.

10. The father of a fool does not have this (Proverbs 17:21). (a) Money, (b) Fame, (c) Children, (d) Joy.

11. Though he wasn't the biological father of Jesus this man could be called the "Father of Jesus." What was his name? (Luke 3:23) (a) Zechariah, (b) Benjamin, (c) Joseph, (d) none of the above.

12. One father whose child was healed by Jesus cried out, "Lord, I believe, help my..." (Mark 9:24) What's the missing word? (a) child, (b) wife, (c) good works, (d) unbelief, (e) tiredness.

13. In the resurrection account who was the Father of (Mark 15:21) Alexander and Rufus? (a) Simon Peter, (b) Simon Magnus, (c) Simon of Cyrene, (d) Simon Zealotes.

14. This person is sometimes referred to as the "father of lies." (John 8:4) His name is (a) Herod, (b) Pontius Pilate, (c) the devil, (d) Caiaphas.

15. In his book James refers to God as the (James 1:17) (a) father of the Law, (b) father of the Gospel, (c) father of good works, (d) father of lights.

ANSWERS: *(1) a-Adam, (2) b-Jubal, (3) b-Ishmael, (4) d-he would be the father of many nations, (5) c-Jacob, (6) b-Moses, (7) c-Solomon, (8)* *a-Mordecai, (9) c-father of the fatherless, (10) d-joy, (11) c-Joseph, (12) d-unbelief, (13) c-Simon of Cyrene, (14) c-the devil, (15) d-father of lights*

SCORING: 15 Correct: Hail to the chief!; 14 Correct: How does it feel to be next in line to the leader?: 13 Correct: Not quite the father of our "world"; 12 Correct: Do you need a recount?

Prisons and Prisoners In the Bible

(There are many prison ministries in our world today. Some of the characters of the Bible faced stays in prison or were imprisoned for their faith. See if you can determine the character or situation being described. If you need help, a Bible reference is given, but if the book title would give away the answer, only the number reference is given.)

1. My brothers had me sold into slavery and when I refused the advances of my slave master's wife I ended up in prison in Egypt. Who am I? (Genesis 39:11-20) (a) Abraham, (b) Joseph, (c) Paul, (d) Jacob, (e) none of the above.

2. I was with Paul and imprisoned in Philippi during a missionary journey. Paul and I led songs and prayers in the night and impressed the Roman jailer when we did not escape during a prison destroying earthquake. Who am I? (Acts 16:25-31) (a) Barnabas, (b) Mark, (c) Silas, (d) Felix, (e) Festus.

3. I faced the most famous prisoner in the history of the world but I did not understand this at the time. The Roman governor sent this man, Jesus, to me and I tried to entice him to perform a miracle but He refused. Who am I? (Luke 23:6-12) (a) Pontius Pilate, (b) Caiaphas, (c) Annas, (d) Herod, (e) None of the above.

4. My husband had a famous prisoner who was incarcerated because he spoke against me and my husband and my former husband. My daughter's wicked dance helped me to fix this prisoner, John, for good. Who am I? (Mark 6:14-29) (a) Herodias, (b) Bathsheba, (c) Mary Magdalene, (d) Salome, (e) Bernice.

5. I was put in a prison cell in Jerusalem (and also in stocks and in a cistern) but these weren't the only times I was detained for my faith and my prophetic proclamations. I angered the king and the religious leaders and the people

too but I kept trying to serve God. Who am I? (37:16-21) (a) Isaiah, (b) Jeremiah, (c) Hosea, (d) Daniel, (e) Moses.

6. Though I was never in prison I always seemed to be hiding from an insane king, from some of my own people, and even from my rebellious son who tried to steal away my kingship. Who am I? (II Samuel 15-18) (a) Saul, (b) Solomon, (c) David, (d) Absalom, (e) Hezekiah.

7. I was the last king of Israel and I was arrested and imprisoned in the king's palace. My early incarceration changed as the conquering king later allowed me to eat at his table. Who am I? (II Samuel 25:27-30) (a) David, (b) Hezekiah, (c) Uzziah, (d) Jehoiachin, (e) Josiah.

8. Though not placed in prison I wasn't imprisoned but I was banished to the island of Patmos for speaking against the powers that be. Who am I? (Revelation 1:9-11) (a) John, (b) Paul, (c) James, (d) Silas, (e) Judas.

9. My name is Paul and I wrote several letters while sitting in prison. My "epistle of joy," written during my confinement, is a book that shows my faith. What is the name of this book written to a helpful people? (1:3-8) (a) Romans, (b) Titus, (c) Philippians, (d) Mark, (e) Jude.

10. I was called a "notorious prisoner" in the Bible and I ended up being released from prison instead of Jesus by the Roman governor because of cries of support from the stirred up crowd. Who am I? (Matthew 27:15-22) (a) Pontius Pilate, (b) Herod Antipas, (c) Simon bar Jonah, (d) Barabbas, (e) Ananias.

11. I ended up in a prison of my own making, the belly of a whale! My name is Jonah and God caused a great fish to swallow me because I refused to preach a message of repentance and destruction to a great ancient city. What is the name of that city? (Jonah 1:1-17) (a) Jerusalem, (b) Nineveh, (c) Tarsus, (d) Bethlehem, (e) Rome.

12. King Herod killed James, the brother of John and had me arrested and imprisoned but an angel helped me

escape. Who am I? (Acts 12:1-11) (a) Philip, (b) Thomas (c) Nathanael, (d) Peter, (e) Paul.

ANSWERS: *1 (B), 2 (C), 3 (D), 4 (A), 5 (B), 6 (C), 7 (D), 8 (A), 9 (C), 10 (D), 11 (B), 12 (D).*

SCORING: 12 or 11 correct: Nothing is shackling you from finding the answers; 10 or 9 correct: You must have time on your hands; 8 or fewer correct: Spend some solitary time studying even more.

Problems in the Bible

(Are the people of God "free" from problems? Ideally, it would seem that they should be, yet often they are not. Faith is sometimes tested and problems for God's people can be an opportunity to grow in faith. See if you can guess the "problem" situation or person or place from the Old Testament being described in the brief clue. Check the Bible reference if you need more help.)

1. The place of the first *problem* of sin. (Genesis 2:15, 3:6-7)
2. A wet solution to the *problem* of wickedness. (Genesis 7:17, 21)
3. Abram's *problem* nephew. (Genesis 13:7)
4. A *problem* maid, at least for Sarah. (Genesis 21:9)
5. A *problem* arose when this man got the wrong bride. (Genesis 29:21-25)
6. This dreamer was a *problem* for his brothers. (Genesis 37:5)
7. This man created *problem*s for himself by secretly killing an Egyptian persecuting a fellow countryman. (Exodus 2:11-12)
8. This man had a *problem* with a hardened heart. (Exodus 7:13)
9. These people voiced their *problem* to Moses. (Exodus 14:10-11)
10. To solve the *problem* of a lack of bread this heavenly food was given (Exodus 16:15)
11. This man helped Moses solve the *problem* of getting better organized. (Exodus 18:12-17ff.)
12. God's people caused *problem*s for themselves by building this evil idol. (Exodus 32:1-4)
13. This woman developed the *problem* of leprosy by rebelling against her brother's leadership. (Numbers 12:10)

14. A *problem* of the lack of faith developed in God's people when they heard the report of these men. (Numbers 13-14)
15. This *problem* man and his followers were swallowed up by the earth. (Numbers 16:32)
16. By striking this object in anger and without giving God the glory, Moses created grave *problem*s for himself. (Numbers 20:11-12)
17. This man had a *problem* with a talking donkey, the only time in the Bible an animal "speaks." (Numbers 22:21-28)
18. A *problem* of walls in this city was overcome with trumpets and faith. (Joshua 6:1, 20)
19. The *problem* of this man's greed led to *problem*s for all of God's people. (Joshua 7:1)
20. This man made a *problem* vow. (Judges 11:30, 35)
21. This strong man had a *problem* of talking too much to the wrong person. (Judges 16:15-20)
22. The *problem* of this priest was his two evil sons. (I Samuel 2:12)
23. The *problem* of King Saul was his pride and the fact that he usurped priestly duties. (I Samuel 13:8-11)
24. Adultery was the *problem* David shared with this woman. (II Samuel 11:2-4)
25. This son of David with his flowing hair created nothing but *problem*s for his father and others. (II Samuel 15:1-10)

ANSWERS: *(1) Eden, (2) Flood, (3) Lot, (4) Hagar, (5) Jacob, (6) Joseph, (7) Moses, (8) Pharaoh, (9) Israel, (10) Manna, (11) Jethro, (12) Golden Calf, (13) Miriam, (14) Spies, (15) Korah, (16) Rock, (17) Balaam, (18) Jericho, (19) Achan, (20) Jephthah, (21) Samson, (22) Eli, (23) Sacrificing, (24) Bathsheba, (25) Absalom*

SCORING: 25 or 24 correct: This quiz was no problem for you; 23 or 22 correct: Not many problems when you took this quiz; 21 or 20 correct: You solved these problems one by one; Less than 20 correct: No problem when you keep reading the Bible!

"St. Patrick and Saints in the Bible"

(St. Patrick's Day is March 17. He is one of scores of "saints" recognized in the church. The word often translated as "saint," especially in the King James Version of the Bible, is the word for "holy one" or one who is "separate" from the "regular" people of the world. The word has been adopted by the church to refer to exemplary individuals who live or share their faith. In today's "quiz" we share a few thoughts about Patrick and then about Biblical "saints." Check the Biblical reference if you need help. If the book reference gives away the name of the writer or situation, the book reference is not given.)

1. My name is Patrick and it is said that I drove the following out of Ireland: (a) Infidels, (b) Snakes, (c) Those who hated green, (d) non-Trinitarian believers.

2. In my teaching in Ireland sometimes I (Patrick) would hold up a shamrock and challenge my hearers by saying, (a) We need to go green, (b) We need this clover to feed our flocks, (c) Is it one leaf or three?, (d) Is this a lot of blarney?

3. In my thirteen letters in the New Testament I often used the word "saint" to describe the people and congregations I was writing to. Who am I? *(Romans 1:7)* (a) Peter, (b) John, (c) Paul, (d) Mark, (e) None of the above.

4. In the book of Revelation the prayers of the saints are compared with *(Revelation 5:8)* (a) incense, (b) scrolls, (c) fruit, (d) wine.

5. Though this famous Biblical character, the "seventh from Adam," did not write any books Jude says that he prophesied about thousands of saints or holy ones. *(Jude 1:14)* What is his name? (a) Cain, (b) Enoch, (c) Noah, (d) Melchizedek

6. According to Matthew's Gospel the bodies of saints which were dead came to life during this situation. What

situation is Matthew describing *(Matthew 27:52)?* (a) Christ's transfiguration, (b) Christ's birth, (c) Christ's Baptism, (d) Christ's resurrection, (e) None of the above.

7. Acts 9 finds this prophet arguing with God about His use of a certain person to preach the Gospel. He talks about the "harm" that this man, Saul, had brought upon the saints. Who is this prophet *(Acts 9:13)?* (a) John the Baptist, (b) Ananias, (c) Barnabas, (d) Silas, (e) None of the above.

8. In the 7th chapter of this Old Testament book this prophet of the exile in Babylon mentions God's "saints" several times. This same prophet is also quoted in the New Testament by Jesus and also in the book of Revelation. What is his name? (a) Jeremiah, (b) Ezekiel, (c) Daniel, (d) Samuel, (e) Jonah.

9. This man describes himself as the "least of all the saints" in Ephesians 3:8. Who is this Biblical writer? (a) Paul, (b) Peter, (c) Luke, (d) Apollos.

10. According to I Corinthians 6:2 the "saints" will assist with this important task in the history of the world: (a) They will gather people into heaven, (b) They will stand guard at the Tree of Life, (c) They will judge the world, (d) They will care for the streets of gold in heaven.

11. The King James Version in Psalm 106:16 calls these two Old Testament individuals "saints." Who are they? (a) Abraham and Isaac, (b) Jacob and Judah, (c) David and Solomon, (d) Moses and Aaron.

12. The book of Psalms is the hymn book of the Old Testament. It describes that the following is "precious" to God *(Psalm 116:15):* (a) the death of His "saints," (b) the preaching of His "saints," (c) The conquest of His "saints," (d) The naming of His "saints," (e) the birth of His "saints".

13. In his letter to Timothy the Apostle Paul describes the loving acts of widows who serve in the church could include this *(I Timothy 5:10):* (a) being well-known

for good deeds, (b) bringing up children, (c) showing hospitality, (d) washing the feet of saints, (e) helping those in trouble, (f) all of the above.

14. Sometimes it appears that evil is winning. Revelation 17:6 describes a scene of evil in which an apostate female is (a) drunk with the blood of the saints, (b) putting saints in prison, (c) having saints beheaded, (d) desecrating churches of the saints.

ANSWERS: *(1) b/Snakes; (2) c/Is it one leaf or three? (3) c/Paul; (4) a/ incense; (5) b/Enoch, (6) d/Christ's Resurrection, (7) b/Ananias; (8) c/ Daniel; (9) a/Paul; (10) c/They will judge the world; (11) d/Moses and Aaron; (12) a/the death of His "saints"; (13) f/all of the above; (14) a/drunk with the blood of the saints.*

SCORING: 14 correct – You are a knowledgeable "saint"!; 13 or 12 correct – You know a great deal about God's saints or holy ones; 11 or 10 correct – You, like many other saints, have been tested; 9 or fewer correct – Being a saint is not based on what we know but on our faith!

School in the Bible

(School is an important part of life and not just for children and young adults. Churches also have Sunday School and religion programs. You may grade yourself with this quiz. If you need help, check the Biblical reference.)

1. As a youth, my parents once lost track of me in the city of Jerusalem. Days later they found me in the temple speaking with the teachers and doctors. I proved that Godly wisdom is more important than just knowing facts. Who am I? *(Luke 2:41-52)*

2. When I was young I studied at the feet of a great Jewish teacher named Gamaliel. Many years later I persecuted Christians. Finally, I was converted and became a Christian who preached to the Gentiles. I wrote 13 books of the Bible and ended up teaching many people. Who am I? *(Acts 22:3)*

3. When I was a youth I saw a vision of the Lord in the temple at Jerusalem. I became an Old Testament prophet of the Lord. Once during my life I was thrown into a pit. At another time I wore a yoke--the same type that oxen wore as an "object lesson" in teaching about coming oppression. I can't give you the title of the book where I am found because it would give away my name. Who am I? *(1:4-11)*

4. I was a young tiller of the ground. I grew many vegetables but I was very rebellious against God. My brother was a keeper of sheep. One day I became very angry with him and I killed him. I hadn't learned the proper lessons. Who am I? *(Genesis 4:2-15)*

5. Because I was a precocious youth I was thrown into a pit by my 11 brothers. Later on they sold me into slavery in Egypt. Many years later God led me to interpret one of Pharaoh's dreams and I became a great ruler, next to

the Pharaoh. Later I also forgave my brothers for their sin against me. We all learned many lessons. Who am I? *(Genesis 37:12-36)*

6. When I was young I grew up with my mother and a lady named Eunice. They taught me the word of God. Many years later I became a pastor. The Apostle Paul helped me in my work. In fact, he wrote two letters to me which are part of the Bible. Who am I? *(I Corinthians 4:17)*

7. Even before birth I was chosen by God to lead my people out of slavery. While still a baby the daughter of the leader of Egypt, the Pharaoh, took me into her house and raised me like one of her own, teaching me many things. Many years later I led the people of Israel out of Egypt. Who am I? *(Exodus 2:1-10)*

8. As a youth I became the new king of Israel. As the new king I tried to improve the country of Israel by driving out those people who worshipped idols and teaching from the book of the Law. Not too many people know my name, but I'll give you a hint. It starts with a "J" and it has 6 letters. Who am I? *(II Kings 22:2-28)*

9. When I was young my father, Abraham, took me up into a mountain. He told me that we were going to pray, but later on I discovered that God had told him to sacrifice me on an altar. Actually, it was just a test for my father, and he did not have to sacrifice me. God knew that Abraham was a faithful man. Who am I? *(Genesis 22:1-14)*

10. I was a young adult when I had a vision of God descending from heaven on a ladder. God also promised that I would be one of the ancestors of the Messiah. What an incredible lesson! Who am I? *(Genesis 28:10-22)*

11. As a young girl, I became engaged to a much older man. Before we were married the Holy Spirit came to me and told me that I would have a child from God, even though I wasn't married. Later on, this child became the Savior of the world. It taught me that God is in charge of our lives. Who am I? *(Luke 1:26-38)*

12. When I was quite young I heard God speak to me while I was sleeping in bed. He spoke several times and finally I said, "Speak, Lord, your servant is listening." Years later I taught as one of God's great Old Testament prophets. I can't give you the Bible book reference because the book bears my name. Who am I? *(3:1-10)*

ANSWERS: *(1) Jesus, (2) Saul or Paul, (3) Jeremiah, (4) Cain, (5) Joseph, (6) Timothy, (7) Moses, (8) Josiah, (9) Isaac, (10) Jacob, (11) Mary, (12) Samuel*

SCORING: All Correct—You are ready for school. Nine correct: You have great retention and will not be retained. Eight correct: You do not need to start over. Seven or less correct: Time to hit the books and the "Book"!

"Shadows In The Bible"

(February 2 is Ground Hog Day in Punxsutawny, Pennsylvania, a contrived celebration in which the shadow of a ground hog suggests how many more weeks before spring begins. If the Ground Hog sees his shadow he returns to his burrow for six more weeks. In the pages of the Bible the idea of a shadow is far more profound. See if you can determine the Biblical character or event being described in these events on "Shadows in the Bible." If you need help, check the Biblical reference.)

1. I lived in a very wicked city and part of twin cities which were about to be destroyed. When the evil men of my city tried to accost some holy visitors who visited me I protected them because them came under the "shadow of my roof" (Genesis 19:8, King James Version) Who am I? (a) Abraham, (b) Jacob, (c) Lot, (d) Matthew.

2. I ended up being one of the Judges of Israel after my father, Gideon, died. One of my brothers, Jotham, told a pointed parable about the bramble and the trees and how I invited them to be under my shadow. (Judges 9:15). It did not make me a happy leader. Who am I? (a) Abimelech, (b) Samson, (c) Midian, (d), Eglon.

3. I was a great prophet and I invited King Hezekiah in a sign or miracle from God to consider which way the shadow would go on the sun dial would go—backwards or forwards by ten degrees? He chose that it would go backwards and it did, by the grace of God. (II Kings 20:1-3). Who am I? (a) Jeremiah, (b) Isaiah, (c) Ezekiel, (d) Elijah.

4. I was a great King of Israel and toward the end of my life I prayed a great prayer which included thoughts about shadows. I said, "Our days on earth are like a shadow, without hope." (I Chronicles 29:15) Who am I? (a) David, (b) Solomon, (c) Saul, (d) Josiah.

5. My name is Job and I faced much trouble and tribulation. When my three friends came to see me I was so upset that I said, "May darkness and deep shadow claim it once more." (Job 3:5) What was I talking about? (a) The Sabbath Day, (b) The Day of my death, (c) The Passover, (d) The Day of my birth.

6. My name is David and in one of my many psalms I wrote that God should hide me "in the shadow of His wings" (Psalm 17:8). What else did I say in the same verse? (a) Keep me in your heart for a while, (b) Keep me as the apple of your eye, (c) Make me your lamb, (d) all of the above.

7. Psalm 23 speaks about the "valley of the shadow of death" (Psalm 23:4). In this same chapter written by me, King David, I spoke of (a) a bulwark, (b) an eagle, (c) a rod and staff, (d) all of the above, (e) none of the above.

8. My name is Isaiah and in my book of prophecy I spoke about the birth of the Messiah. I spoke about living "in the shadow of death" (Isaiah 9:2) but in the same verse I also spoke about "walking in _____." What is the missing word? (a) Light, (b) Memphis, (c) Jerusalem, (d) darkness, (e) none of the above.

9. When miracles were rampant in the Holy Land some people were so excited about what was going on that they were hoping that my shadow might fall upon them (Acts 5:15). Who am I? (a) Jesus, (b) Paul, (c) Peter, (d) Barnabas.

10. I wrote that no one should judge Jewish or Gentile Christians by what they do or don't do in faith. I said that these are "a shadow of the things to come." (Colossians 2:17) Who am I? (a) Paul, (b) Peter, (c) Timothy, (d) John, (e) Jude.

ANSWERS: (1) c, (2) a, (3) b, (4) a, (5) d, (6) b, (7) c, (8) d, (9) c, (10) a.

SCORING: If you have 10 correct, you did well. Don't be scared. If you got 9 correct, perhaps you were briefly blinded. If you have 8 correct, check to see if your shadow is still there. If you got 7 or fewer correct, hide the paper and try another quiz.

Sheep and Shepherds in the Bible

(Since the people of the Bible were very tied to their land and ground, much of the imagery of the Bible refers to land and animals and especially to the imagery of sheep and shepherds. In the church the Fourth Sunday of Easter is also known as "Good Shepherd Sunday," a Sunday in which the imagery of Jesus as the Good Shepherd is relished and celebrated. It is also a time when our nation focuses on the stewardship of soil and natural resources. Take this quiz on sheep and shepherds in the Bible and see if you can master this imagery.)

1. All of the following in the Bible took care of sheep except for (Genesis 4:2) (a) Abel, (b) Joseph, (c) David, (e) Cain, (f) Rachel.

2. Abraham was asked by God to sacrifice His son, Isaac, and when Isaac asked his father where the lamb would come from Abraham said (Genesis 22:7-8), (a) "You, son, are the lamb", (b) "God will provide Himself a lamb," (c) (Seeing a goat he said,) "We can use a goat instead" (d) "I am the shepherd and you are the lamb."

3. The Passover ceremony required that a lamb without blemish would be used in the following way (Exodus 12:5-8): (a) it would be allowed to escape into the wilderness, (b) it was to lead the people out of slavery as they followed the lamb, (c) the blood of the slain lamb was to be put on the sides and top of the door, (d) all of the above, (e) none of the above.

4. This man who became king was the "smallest" in his family and contented himself to take care of sheep. What was the name of this shepherd boy who was destined to become king? (I Samuel 16:9-13) (a) Saul, (b) David, (c) Solomon, (d) Amminadab.

5. This priest confronted King David concerning his sin with Bathsheba and did it by telling a parable story about

a man with a lamb whose neighbor seizes his lamb and serves it as a meal (II Samuel 12:1-7). This man was named (a) Melchizedek, (b) Eli, (c) Samuel, (d) Nathan, (e) Zechariah.

6. When the fortunes of Job were restored after his debate or argument with God Job found (Job 42:12) (a) he had half as many sheep as he did at the beginning, (b) he had the same among of sheep as he did at the beginning, (c) he had half again as many sheep as he did at the beginning, (d) he had twice as many sheep as he did at the beginning.

7. In the Twenty Third Psalm David writes all of the following about the shepherd *except* (a) he makes me lie down in green pastures, (b) he leads me besides still waters, (c) he dies for me, (d) he restores my soul, (e) he leads me.

8. In his love poem Solomon wrote of his love that (Song of Solomon 6:6), (a) her teeth were like a flock of sheep, (b) her hair was as soft as the wool of a sheep, (c) her voice was like the bleating of a sheep, (d) her face was as soft and delicate as a lamb.

9. In his prophecy Isaiah writes that (Isaiah 53:6-7) (a) the Messiah was like a lamb led to slaughter (b) like a sheep, the Messiah was silent before its shearers (c) we, like sheep, have all gone astray, (d) all of the above, (e) none of the above.

10. This sign of the peaceful kingdom of the future (Isaiah 65:25) showed that the lamb and this animal would be together: (a) Wolf, (b) Bear, (c) Snake, (d) Goat.

11. Chapter 34 of the book of Ezekiel tells (a) how to butcher sheep, (b) about a prophecy against Israel's shepherds, (c) the difference between sheep and goats, (d) where sheep are to be led to graze.

12. In one of His teaching sermons Jesus asks (Matthew 18:12) (a) whether or not a shepherd with ten sheep will search for two, (b) whether or not a shepherd with 22 sheep will leave them all to fend for themselves, (c) whether a

shepherd with 100 will leave 99 unattended to find or rescue one sheep, (d) whether or not a shepherd can feed a flock with five loaves and two small fish.

13. In one of His teachings in Matthew 25:31ff. Jesus says (a) the people will be separated into groups of sheep and goats, (b) the sheep will be on the left hand, (c) the goats will be killed, (d) all of the above, (e) none of the above.

14. Jesus calls Himself the Good Shepherd in John 10 and says, (a) "He calls his own sheep by name", (b) "The good shepherd lays down his life for the sheep," (c) "I know my own and my own know me," (d) "I have other sheep that are not of this fold," (e) all of the above, (f) none of the above.

15. This man told his fallen disciple, "Feed my lambs" (John 21:15) The man who said this was (a) Simon Peter, (b) Doubting Thomas, (c) Jesus, (d) John, Son of Zebedee.

ANSWERS: *(1) e-Cain; (2) b-"God will provide Himself a lamb"; (3) c-the blood of the slain lamb was to be put on the sides and top of the door; (4) b-David; (5) d-Nathan; (6) d-he had twice as many sheep as he did at the beginning; (7) c-he dies for me; (8) a-here teeth were like a flock of sheep (!); (9) d-all of the above; (10) a-wolf; (11) b-about a prophecy against Israel's shepherds; (12) c-whether a shepherd with 100 will leave 99 unattended to find or rescue one sheep; (13) a-the people will be separated into groups of sheep and goats; (14) e-all of the above; (15) c-Jesus.>*

SCORING: 15 correct – Excellent! No one can pull the wool over your eyes! Jump or leap for joy about a perfect score! 14-13 correct – You hear the Lord's voice and follow Him!; 12-11 correct – Not Baaaad!; 10 or fewer correct – Keep counting your sheep and learning about the Lord!

Summer in the Bible

(The Bible occasionally talks about the seasons of spring, summer, fall and winter. With summer just two days away we offer this "quiz" about the season of summer. See if you can determine the answer by using the clues. Check the Bible reference if you need help. References which would give the answer away do not include the name of the book.)

1. In this Biblical book God makes a promise that as long as the earth endures seedtime and harvest, cold and heat and summer and winter will not cease (8:22). This book is (a) Genesis, (b) Psalms, (c) Matthew, (d) Revelation.
2. The writer of the book of Proverbs suggests that a person should consider this living being as an example in life (Proverbs 6:6-8). He is referring to the (a) grasshopper, (b) Leviathan, (c) ant, (d) caterpillar.
3. A left handed Judge had a special message for the evil ruler named Eglon who had harassed his people. As Eglon sat in his "summer house" this man delivered a message that ended in Eglon's death. (Judges 3:20ff.) The Judge's name was (a) Samson, (b) Jephthah, (c) Gideon, (d) Ehud.
4. In Proverbs 26:1 the writer says that "like snow in summer or rain in harvest" this is something not fitting for a fool: (a) food, (b) honor, (c) justice, (d) wealth.
5. This farmer prophet who focused on social action presented a message to people in an area where he did not live. He decried their wealth and made fun of their "summer houses" which were adorned with wealthy accoutrements. This prophet's name was (a) Elijah, (b) Amos, (c) Malachi, (d) John the Baptist.
6. Jesus talked about this tree and how a person needs to observe the flowering of this tree as a person looks at life and the world. He said that "as soon as its twigs get tender and its leaves come out, you know that summer is near."

(Mark 13:28) This tree is the (a) apple tree, (b) banana tree, (c) fig tree, (d) tree of life.

7. This weeping prophet uses many illustrations about the seasons and especially about summer. During his lifetime this prophet saw himself in stocks and mired in a pit. What is his name? (a) Jeremiah, (b) Ezekiel, (c) Daniel, (d) Jonah.

8. In Psalm 74:17 the writer talks about God setting the boundaries of the earth and making summer and (a) winter, (b) spring, (c) autumn, (d) all of the above.

9. The writer of the book of Proverbs compares a wise and foolish son who gathers crops in the summer but sleeps during (Proverbs 10:5) (a) the winter, (b) mealtime, (c) the harvest, (d) wedding ceremony.

10. In railing against the people of Cush or Egypt Isaiah the prophet warns that wild animals will feed on the people all winter and this will feed on them all summer: (Isaiah 18:6): (a) jackals, (b) people, (c) fish, (d) birds.

ANSWERS: *(1) a/Genesis, (2) c/ant, (3) d/Ehud, (4)b/honor, (5) b/Amos, (6)c/fig tree, (7) a/Jeremiah, (8)a/winter, (9)c/the harvest, (10) d/birds.*

SCORING: 9 or 10 correct—you are very hot! 7 or 8 correct—it will be a long summer. Less than 6 correct—spend some time this summer with a really good book…"the" Book!

Swimming in the Bible

(Swimming is an enjoyable summer sport. Can you guess the "swimmer" or situation being described? The answers follow. If you need help you can check the Bible reference.)

1. I was the first "swimmer" mentioned in the Bible, but I really didn't swim in the traditional sense. I "moved" or "swam" along the "face" of the waters. Who am I? (a) Adam, (b) Spirit, (c) Dinosaur, (d) Eve. See Genesis 1:2

2. We were ungodly people who "missed the boat." We tried to swim but had a difficult time "treading 40 days and 40 nights of water. Who are we? (a) Dinosaurs, (b) People of Babel, (c) People at time of Noah, (d) Nephilim. See Genesis 7

3. I ended up swimming on a meeting with Jesus. He said to me as He was on the water, "Come." I tried to walk on water but my fear led to a sinking feeling. Who am I? (a) Simon Peter, (b) Simon the Zealot, (c) Simon the Tanner, (d) Simon Magnus. See Matthew 14:29-31

4. I was in a shipwreck and the soldiers guarding me and other prisoners wanted to put us to death rather than letting us swim for shore. By God's power, I talked them out of this terrible idea. Who am I? (a) Jonah, (b) Simon Peter, (c) John, (d) Apostle Paul. See Acts 17:42-44

5. When I was in a boat at sea the people were afraid in a storm. I told them that the storm was my fault and that they should throw me in the water to see if I could swim. Strangely enough, they took my advice and something fishy happened to me. Who am I? (a) Jonah, (b) Simon Peter, (c) John, (d) Apostle Paul. See Jonah 1:11-16

6. My name is Jesus. I let this man baptize me in the Jordan River. It wasn't exactly swimming, but I got wet so that I could fulfill the Scriptures. Who was the man who

baptized me? (a) Apostle John, (b) John the Baptist, (c) Philip, (d) Simon the Zealot. See Matthew 3:13-17

7. This book in the Bible talks about the sea turning to blood. It wouldn't be a great place to swim. Name the book. (a) Daniel, (b) Ezekiel, (c) Revelation, (d) Zechariah. See Revelation 16:3

8. My name is Jesus. I said that anyone who causes a little person to sin against God should have one of these tied around his neck. It would not be easy to swim like this. What am I referring to? (a) Millstone, (b) Yoke, (c) Tree, (d) Zion the rock See Matthew 18:6

9. We tried to walk across the divided Red Sea but when the waters came back together we had trouble swimming. Who are we? (a) People of Israel, (b) People of Judah, (c) Pharaoh's army, (d) People of Edom. See Exodus 14:26-28

10. I wasn't exactly talking about swimming but I asked Job, "Who shut up the seas behind doors?" Who am I? (a) God, (b) Devil, (c) Leviathan, (d) Bildad. See Job 38:8-11

11. My name is Jesus. I said that if a person had enough faith he could make one of these be cast into water and swim in the sea. What was I talking about? (a) Grain of Mustard seed, (b) Rock, (c) coin, (d) mountain. See Mark 11:23

12. I told Nicodemus that he needed to be born of water and the spirit. Perhaps this is a little like swimming with both body and mind. Who am I? (a) Herod Antipas, (b) John, (c) Jesus, (d) Paul See John 3:3-7

13. I wasn't a swimmer but Jesus talked to me about "living water." I wonder how that would be for swimming. Who am I? (a) Naaman, (b) Samaritan woman, (c) Mary Magdalene, (d) Mary, wife of Clopas. See John 4:11-14

14. I was told by the prophet Elisha that I should swim seven times in the Jordan River and I would be cured of leprosy. Who am I? (a) Naaman, (b) Elijah, (c) Jezebel, (d) Ahab. See II Kings 5:1-14

15. This piece of carpentry equipment went swimming in the time of Elisha but sunk to the bottom. Later it learned to

float. What was it? (a) Boat, (b) Ruler, (c) axe head, (d) yoke. See II Kings 6:1-7

16. When I faced the prophets of Baal, God told me to make the altar and sacrifices to God swim in the water to prove His power. God eventually burned everything up to prove His power. Who am I? (a) Noah, (b) Abraham, (c) Lot, (d) Elijah. See I Kings 18:30-38

17. In my prophecy I was called the "Son of Man" and God showed me a deep river that no one could swim in. Who am I? (a) Jeremiah, (b) Micah, (c) Ezekiel, (d) Malachi. See Ezekiel 47:3-6

18. In my day the Pharaoh ordered that the babies be thrown into the water, even though they couldn't swim. My mother put me in a floating basket to save my life. Who am I? (a) Moses, (b) Aaron, (c) Miriam, (d) Jochebed See Exodus 2:1-10

19. In my prophecy I spoke about "peace being like a river." I guess that you could swim in such a river. My other famous prophecy talks about the "prince of peace." Who am I? (a) Jonah, (b) Isaiah, (c) Elijah, (d) Elisha. See Isaiah 66:12

20. We once swam but in the Bible we were dead when Jesus performed a miracle to feed 5,000 people using us. What are we? (a) Two fish, (b) dinosaurs, (c) Leviathan, (d) dogs. See Matthew 14:17-21

ANSWERS: *(1) (b) Holy Spirit, (2) (c) People in Noah's time, (3) (a) Simon Peter, (4) (d) Apostle Paul, (5) (a) Jonah, (6) (b) John the Baptist, (7) (c) Revelation, (8) (a) Millstone, (9) (c) Pharaoh's armies, (10) (a) God, (11) (d) Mountain, (12) (c) Jesus, (13) (b) Samaritan woman at the well, (14) (a) Naaman, (15) (c) axe head, (16) (d) Elijah, (17) (c) Ezekiel, (18) (a) Moses, (19) (b) Isaiah, (20) (a) Two fish*

SCORING; One or two wrong—You are "swimming" with the best; Three or four wrong—Keep working on your back stroke; five or six wrong—Perhaps you will soon be at the next level; more than six wrong—Don't swim alone!

Taxes in the Bible

(Most of us do not need to be reminded that April 15, is "Tax Day." Some pay their taxes on time while others wait until the last minute. Either way, we know that they must be paid. Benjamin Franklin said, "There is nothing more certain than death and taxes." Taxes are even "found" in the Bible. See if you can relate to taxes in the Bible using this little quiz. If you need some help, check the Biblical reference.)

1. King Rehoboam in great foolishness (I Kings 12:8-11) rejected the advice of his "elders" and imposed even heavier taxation on the people than did his father. His father's name was (a) Herod, (b) David, (c) Solomon, (d) Nebuchadnezzar.

2. In the closing days of the kings of Judah (II Kings 23:35) this person levied stiff taxes to keep the people in subjection: (a) King David,(b) Pharaoh Neco, (c) King Herod,(d) Melchizedek.

3. In a God-blessed program to save the country of Egypt the Pharaoh's main helper (Genesis 41:46-57) imposed a type of taxation in which he saved up the grain for a future famine. Pharaoh's helper was named (a) Abraham, (b) Solomon, (c) Jacob, (d) Joseph, (e) Isaiah.

4. The reason why Joseph took his family to Bethlehem near the time of the birth of Jesus (Luke 2:1-3) was for (a) the census for tax purposes (b) the family to be close to relatives (c) business purposes to make investments (d) sight-seeing and to get away from nosy neighbors.

5. In comparing Jesus with John the Baptist the critics of Jesus (Matthew 11:19) called Him (a) a glutton, (b) a drunkard, (c) a friend of tax collectors, (d) a friend of sinners, (e) all of the above.

6. When Jesus and Peter needed to pay their tax (Matthew 17:24-27) Jesus told Peter (a) not to pay the tax as a protest,

(b) to see Judas and get some money for the tax, (c) to go fishing and find a coin for taxes in the fish's mouth, (d) to protest the tax and not pay it.

7. When Jesus was confronted with loyalty to the government or to God (Matthew 22:17-21) He said, "Render unto _____ the things that are 'his.'" The missing word(*s*) is/are (a) the taxman, (b) Caesar, (c) God, (d) b and c in separate phrases.

8. One of the most famous tax collectors in the New Testament (Mark 2:14) was (a) Mark, (b) Judas Thaddeus, (c) Judas Iscariot, (d) Levi.

9. In a famous Pentecost sermon (Acts 5:37) a sermon or message mentions Judas the Galilean who led a revolt during the "census" or "taxing" (King James Version). This man who gave this message was (a) Paul, (b) Barnabas, (c) Peter, (d) Stephen.

10. Paul wrote about taxes (Romans 13:7) that (a) we should not pay them as a protest, (b) we should use trickery to avoid paying as much tax as possible, (c) if you owe tax, pay tax, (d) being a tax collector was the unforgivable sin.

ANSWERS: (1) C, (2) B, (3) D, (4) A, (5) E, (6) C, (7) D, (8) D, (9) C, (10) C.

SCORING: If you score 1 or 2 wrong, you are probably ready to pay your taxes. If you score 3 or 4 wrong, you may need to have someone loan you their Bible dictionary. If you score more than 5 wrong, you may have taxes due!

Thanksgiving in the Bible

(Thanksgiving is one of the oldest holidays in human existence. Again and again in the pages of the Bible, God and His people talk about the need to be thankful. Complete this Bible quiz on "thanks" and "thanksgiving." If you need help with the questions, consider the Biblical reference. If the verse would give away the answer only the passage is given and not the name of the book.)

1. I wrote to my favorite congregation and said, "I thank my God every time I remember you." Who am I? (1:21) (a) Moses to the people (b) Paul to the Philippians (c) John the Baptist to Herod's court (d) John to the Laodiceans.

2. As a "psalmist" or writer of Psalms in describing God in Psalm 95:2 I wrote, "Let us come before Him with" (a) Praises (b) Offerings (c) Fasting (d) thanksgiving (e) none of the above.

3. In Psalm 100:4 I invited people by saying, "Enter his _____ with thanksgiving." The missing word is (a) gates (b) house (c) pastures (d) booth, (e) none of the above.

4. In a letter to a troubled congregation I described this as the "cup of thanks for which we give thanks." (I Corinthians 10:16) What was I talking about? (a) Eucharist (b) Communion (c) Lord's Supper (d) Sacrament of the Altar (e) All of the above.

5. In thankfulness to God for allowing me to rescue my nephew, Lot, from the Canaanites (Genesis 14:18-20) I, Abraham, gave a tithe gift to (a) Kedorlaomer the King (b) Melchizedek the king of Salem (c) Solomon the king of Judah (d) Nebuchadnezzar the king of Babylon, (e) none of the above.

6. When God's people were able to subdue the Philistines at Mizpah I, Samuel, as the priest and Judge set up a stone in

honor of the victory and called it (I Samuel 7:12) (a) Baal (b) Ashtoreth (c) Chronos (d) Ebenezer, (e) Tiny Tim.

7. I am Moses and I led my people for many years. In my farewell speech I related that God was telling His people (Deuteronomy 8) (a) not to forget Him (b) to go back to Egypt (c) to spend 40 more years in the wilderness (d) to adapt themselves as much as possible to the customs of the surrounding nations and thus be people of peace, (e) all of the above.

8. As we, the disciples of Jesus, were on the way to Jerusalem with Him we saw how Jesus healed a group of lepers and the following was what happened (Luke 17:11-91): (a) nine of the ten lepers thanked Him (b) none of the lepers thanked Him (c) the disciples thanked Him (d) a single Samaritan thanked Him. (e) only the Jewish leper thanked Him.

9. My name is Nehemiah, a leader of God's people. As they returned from the Babylonian exile to rebuild the Temple I led the people in giving thanks to God (Nehemiah 12:31) (a) by organizing two choirs to give thanks (b) by conquering ten cities (c) by bringing ten loaves of bread to the Temple (d) by returning to Persia where it was safe, (e) none of the above.

10. In writing to the Thessalonian Christians I (Paul) told them to (I Thessalonians 5:18) (a) spend the day reading their Bibles (b) watch a holy parade (c) give thanks in all circumstances (d) make a large meal and share it with their family, (e) all of the above.

11. In my letter to the Corinthians (I Corinthians 15:57) I (Paul) said that Christians are to give thanks to God for (a) the victory of the Resurrection (b) food and raiment (c) pastors and teachers (d) holy spouses, (e) all of the above.

12. When I wrote to the Romans I (Paul) said that people who know God but do not give thanks to Him (Romans 1:21) (a) are just plain silly (b) know better (c) have foolish dark hearts (d) are doing the right thing.

ANSWERS: *(1) b, (2) a, (3) a, (4) e, (5) b, (6) d, (7) a, (8) d, (9) a, (10) c, (11) a, (12) c*

SCORING: 12 correct – Aren't you thankful that you know what the Bible says about Thanksgiving? 10/11 – correct – We should be thankful for what we know. 9 or fewer correct – We are thankful that we can go back to God's Word at all times for more help!

Thorns in the Bible

(Our nation faces some thorny problems and issues as we deal with the sin of terrorism. "Thorns" are a recurring theme in the pages of the Bible. See if you can identify the Biblical character or other word associated with the thorns being described. If you need help, check the Biblical reference.)

1. This man asked rhetorically whether or not men can gather grapes from thorns. Who was it? (Matthew 7:16)
2. For this man God said that because of sin, the ground would produce thorns and thistles. Who was it? (Genesis 3:18)
3. The soldiers in Pontius Pilate's court made this from thorns and put it on the head of Jesus. What was this object? (Mark 15:17)
4. This author characterized his love as "the lily among thorns." Name this king. (Song of Songs 2:2)
5. Jeremiah, the prophet, warned God's people that because of sin they would sow this but reap thorns. What would they sow? (Jeremiah 12:13)
6. In a parable that Jesus told when this "fell" among thorns it was choked. What was choked? (Matthew 13:7)
7. This wicked king of Judah ended up being captured "among the thorns" by the Assyrian king. Name him. (II Chronicles 33:11)
8. The laughter of this kind of man, according to the author of Ecclesiastes, is like thorns "crackling" under a boiling pot. Describe this man. (Ecclesiastes 7:6)
9. This man had a "thorn in the flesh" that humbled him before God. Name him. (II Corinthians 12:7)
10. Through this man God warned His people that the pagans which were not driven out of the "Promised Land" would become "thorns" in their side. Name this great leader. (Numbers 33:55)

ANSWERS: (1) Jesus, (2) Adam, (3) Crown, (4) Solomon, (5) Wheat, (6) Seed, (7) Manasseh, (8) Fool, (9) Paul, (10) Moses

SCORING: 10 correct: Roses to you!; 9 correct: You didn't get stuck; 8 or fewer Correct: Sort of a thorny problem.

Grain, Harvesting, and Threshing in the Bible

(The Bible contains many references to harvest, threshing, and grains. See if you can determine the answers in this "Threshing Quiz." If you need help, check the Biblical reference. If the Bible reference would give away the answer the book is not given.)

1. Wheat and other grasses were created on this day of the creation (Genesis 1:11-13) (a) first day, (b) second day, (c) third day, (d) fourth day, (e) the Bible doesn't say.
2. I was a "worker of the ground" and was upset when my offering to God was not regarded like my brother's was. In anger I ended his life. Who am I? (Genesis 4:1-8). (a) Abel, (b) Seth, (c) Cain, (d) Lamech.
3. My work in Egypt involved helping the people of the nation have enough food to eat by carefully rationing the grain resources. What was my name? (Genesis 41:46-57). (a) Pharaoh, (b) Abraham, (c) Jacob, (d) Joseph, (e) Judah.
4. In offerings for the Temple the Grain Offering was to be (Leviticus 2:1) (a) "unground" grain, (b) fine flour, (c) flax seed, (d) a mixture of wheat, corn, and barley.
5. When Ruth was with her mother-in-law and working in the field gleaning wheat I urged that my reapers help her by leaving extra grain for her. What was my name? (Ruth 2:14-16) (a) Boaz, (b) Mahlon, (c) Chilion, (d) Obed
6. I urged my daughter-in-law, Ruth, to spend time with her future husband in the area of the threshing floor. What was my name? (Ruth 3:1-5) (a) Orpah (b) Bathsheba (c) Naomi, (d) Rahab
7. In my prophetic Old Testament book written at the time near the fall of Jerusalem I railed against false prophets and quoted the Lord, saying, "What has straw in common with wheat?" My book bears my name. Who am I? (23:28) (a) Isaiah, (b) Jeremiah, (c) Ezekiel, (d) Daniel

8. My name is John the Baptist and I prepared the way for Jesus and said (Matthew 3:12) (a) His winnowing fork is in His hand, (b) He will clear His threshing floor, (c) He will gather His wheat into the barn, (d) He will burn the chaff with unquenchable fire, (e) all of the above.

9. Jesus told these people that "the harvest is plentiful but the laborers are few." Who was He talking to? (Matthew 9:37-38) (a) Pharisees, (b) disciples, (c) the crowd, (d) Herodians, (e) none of the above

10. In an unusual situation in the New Testament Jesus' disciples plucked grain and ate it while going through the grain fields. Why were the Pharisees upset about this? (Matthew 12:1-2) (a) the disciples were working on the Sabbath Day, (b) the disciples were stealing, (c) the disciples would get sick from raw grain, (d) the grain was for the priests, (e) none of the above.

11. In one of the parables of Jesus the servants were warned that you shouldn't pull this up with the wheat? What was He speaking about? (Matthew 13:29) (a) weeds, (b) grass, (c) fruit, (d) worms

12. When Jesus told the parable of the Sower (Mark 4:1-9) He spoke about seed (a) sown on the path, (b) sown on rocky soil, (c) sown among thorns, (d) sown on good soil, (e) all of the above.

13. The Rich Fool in the parable told by Jesus (Luke 12:13-21) (a) was named Dives, (b) died the night of his great harvest, (c) repented when he saw his sin, (d) wanted to hire Lazarus to harvest his crops.

14. Jesus prayed for this man because Satan wanted to "sift him like wheat." Who was this man? (Luke 22:31-32) (a) Judas Iscariot, (b) Herod, (c) Pontius Pilate, (d) Simon Peter, (e) Caiaphas

15. As Jesus was reacting to people's concern about food He said that His food was to do God's will. He also talked about the harvest and said (John 4:31-36), (a) there were four months to the harvest, (b) the fields were white for

harvest, (c) the one who reaps is receiving wages, (d) they were gathering fruit for eternal life, (e) all of the above.

16. I said that "Unless a grain of wheat falls to the earth and dies, it remains alone, but if it dies, it bears much fruit." My name was (John 12:24) (a) Jesus, (b) Nicodemus, (c) Pontius Pilate, (d) Caiaphas, (e) Matthew

17. In my letter to my young friend, Timothy, I said, "You shall not muzzle an ox when it treads out the grain." What was I talking about? (I Timothy 5:18) (a) not harming beasts of burden, (b) paying church workers proper wages, (c) not questioning rules made by secular leaders, (d) not working on the Sabbath Day.

18. My name is James and I wrote about wisdom and said that a harvest of righteousness is sown in (James 3:18) (a) love, (b) peace, (c) joy, (d) patience, (e) all of the above

ANSWERS: *1-(c) third day; 2-(c) Cain, 3-(d) Joseph, 4-(b) fine flour, 5-(a) Boaz, 6-(c) Naomi, 7-(b) Jeremiah, 8-(e) all of the above, 9-(b) disciples, 10-(a) the disciples were working on the Sabbath Day, 11-(a) weeds, 12-(e) all of the above, 13-(b) died the night of his great harvest, 14-(d) Simon Peter, 15-(e) all of the above, 16-(a) Jesus, 17-(b) paying church workers proper wages, 18-(b) peace.*

SCORING: If you had 16-18 correct you know your grain. If you 13-15 correct you are ready for the harvest. If you had less than 13 correct remember that the harvest of reading God's Word is plentiful! Enjoy the bounty!

The Twelve Days of Christmas Revisited

(During the time of the Reformation and Counter Reformation some religious groups in England were not allowed to practice their faith. In response, it is believed that the Christmas carol, "The Twelve Days of Christmas" was composed as a way for some to memorize aspects of their faith. In the "Twelve Days of Christmas" quiz below see if you can see what the number code stood for. In most cases the person learning the code would need to recite a complete answer of the items being sought. In this difficult and coded quiz, most of the answers are legitimate but only one answer is what was used with the "Twelve Days of Christmas." Check the answers at the end to see how you did.)

1. The one partridge in a pear tree stood for (a) a Christmas songbird, (b) Jesus Christ, (c) the cedars of Lebanon, (d) the first book of the Bible.

2. The two turtle doves stood for (a) the Old and New Testaments, (b) the Law and the Gospel, (c) two Christmas trees for the church, (d) day and night.

3. The three French hens stood for (a) the Holy Trinity, (b) Bethlehem, Jerusalem and Nazareth, (c) faith, hope and love, (d) Mary, Joseph and Jesus.

4. The four calling birds were (a) the four corners of the earth, (b) Isaiah, Jeremiah, Ezekiel and Daniel, (c) the four Gospels, Matthew, Mark, Luke and John, (d) the four weeks of Advent.

5. The five golden rings were (a) the five books of Moses or the Torah, (b) the first five kings of Israel, (c) the five major prophets, (d) the five days before Christmas.

6. The six geese a-laying stood for (a) the number of Satan, 6/6/6, (b) Abraham, Isaac and Jacob and Peter, James and John, (c) the first six days of creation, (d) the six chief doctrines of the faith.

7. The seven swans a-swimming stood for the (a) the seven days of creation, (b) the seven gifts of the Holy Spirit, (c) the seven churches of the book of Revelation, (d) the seven most important Judges of Israel.

8. The eight maids a-milking stood for (a) the eight general epistles of the New Testament not written by Paul, (b) the eight beatitudes of Matthew 5, (c) new beginning, (d) Holy Baptism.

9. The nine ladies dancing stood for (a) the nine books of the Bible, beginning with I Kings, (b) the six days of creation added to the number for God (three), (c) the nine fruit of the Holy Spirit—love, joy, peace, patience, kindness, goodness, faithfulness, gentleness, self-control, (d) the nine healed lepers who didn't thank Jesus.

10. The ten lords a-leaping stood for (a) the Ten Commandments, (b) the seven days of creation and the Trinity combined, (c) the ten cities of refuge in the Old Testament, (d) the ten horned beast in the book of Revelation.

11. The eleven pipers piping stood for the (a) eleven Judges of the book of Judges (b) eleven faithful disciples, excluding Judas (c) the number of new beginnings plus the Trinity, (d) the minor prophets, except for Malachi.

12. The twelve drummers drumming symbolized (a) the twelve disciples, (b) the twelve patriarchs of the Old Testament, (c) the twelve New Testament books authored by the Apostle Paul, (d) the twelve articles of the Apostles Creed.

ANSWERS: *1 (b), 2 (a), 3 (c), 4 (c), 5 (a), 6 (c), 7 (b), 8 (b), 9 (c), 10 (a), 11 (b), 12 (d).*

SCORING: Twelve Correct? Keep singing. Eleven Correct? Leap for joy. Ten Correct? Ten is a perfect number. Nine or fewer correct? Check the lyrics.

Trinity Quiz

(Once a year eight weeks after Easter the church commemorates "Trinity Sunday,", a once a year focus in the church on the concept and idea that God is Triune—a three in one being consisting of Father, Son and Holy Spirit. Many Christian churches will talk about this concept this Sunday and many liturgical churches will also recite the Athanasian Creed, a painstaking defense of the Trinity. How much do you know about the Trinity? Take the quiz below (True or False) and then check the answers at the end to see how you did.)

1. True False   The word "Trinity" is not found in the Bible.

2. True False   Jesus Himself never talked about the Father, Son, and Holy Spirit in the same sentence.

3. True False   At the Baptism of Jesus the three persons of the Trinity are clearly evident and named.

4. True False   The people of the Old Testament did not believe that God was one.

5. True False   The Spirit of God is not mentioned in the Old Testament.

6. True False   Phrases such as "holy, holy, holy" in both the Old and New Testament are hints about God being a Triune being.

7. True False   Many Biblical scholars believe that the "angel of the Lord" mentioned in many places in the Old Testament refer to "Jesus" in the Old Testament.

8. True False   The idea of the Trinity was the invention of Athanasius and the Early Church.

9. True False   The Apostle Paul never talked about the Father, Son, and Holy Spirit in the same sentence.

10. True   False   The Spirit was the one who led Jesus in the
                   wilderness to be tempted.

Here are the answers:

1. *True.* The word "Trinity" and "triune" are not found
   in the Bible but most main stream Christian laity and
   scholars believe that the concept is clearly evident.
2. *False.* In Matthew 28:18-20 Jesus tells us to baptized "in
   the Name of the Father and of the Son and of the Holy
   Spirit."
3. *True.* Matthew 3:3-17 describes Jesus (the Son) standing
   in the water, the dove (the Spirit) coming down from
   heaven and a voice (the Father) affirming that Jesus was
   His beloved Son.
4. *False.* The basic statement of faith of the Jewish people
   affirmed in Deuteronomy 6:4-5 that the "Lord our God
   is one."
5. *False.* The Spirit of God is mentioned in the second verse
   of Genesis where it states that the "Spirit of God was
   hovering over the face of the water (the deep)." (Genesis 1:2)
6. *True.* Examples of this are Isaiah 6:4 and Revelation 4:8
   which state, "Holy, holy, holy is the Lord God Almighty."
7. *True.* One example of this is Genesis 22:11 where "the
   angel of the Lord" stays the hand of Abraham who was
   about to take the life of His promised Son, Isaac.
8. *False.* It was hardly an "invention" of Athanasius and the
   Early Church. The church had studied and debated for
   decades about the unique nature of the Trinity and the
   Triune God. The Athanasian Creed which was adopted
   after the Fourth Century expressed what the church
   taught and believed in opposition to what was called the
   Arian controversy which sought to deny that Jesus was
   true God.
9. *False.* One example of a "Pauline Benediction" which
   spoke about the grace of our Lord Jesus Christ (the Son),

the love of God (the Father), and the Communion of the Holy Spirit (the Spirit). (II Corinthians 13:14)

10. *True.* Matthew 4:1 clearly states that after His Baptism, the Spirit led Jesus into the desert "to be tempted."

SCORING: If you had 9-10 correct you are a "Trinitarian scholar." If you had 7-8 correct you join most of Christendom in studying yet struggling with this difficult concept. If you have 6 or less correct you are forgiven "in the Name of the Father and of the Son and of the Holy Spirit"!

Valentines in the Bible

(St. Valentine's Day is February 14 and people in love say, "Be my valentine.". Tradition says that "Valentine" was a priest of Rome who ministered to martyrs during the persecution of Claudius and who himself was martyred in 270 A.D. He is known as the "patron saint of lovers" since his martyrdom on February 14 is about the time in the New Year when people begin to think of love and marriage. There are many "valentines" or "sweethearts" in the Bible. See if you can name the "valentine" being described. This is a tough quiz! Check the Biblical reference if you need help.)

1. We were the first "valentines" in the Bible and in the world. Who are we? *(Genesis 1-2)*

2. As "sweethearts" or "valentines" we had the joy of being the earthly parents of the long-promised messiah. Who are we? *(Luke 2)*

3. When the Apostle Paul did some of his work on earth we "valentines" helped him make tents. Who are we? *(Acts 18)*

4. One of us had to work 7 years in order to get his "valentine" and then another 7 years after our marriage. Talk about a labor of love! Who are we? *(Genesis 29)*

5. We were "valentines" in the Bible. I was the long-promised son to my father and mother, though when I was a youth my father faced a sacrifice that was surprising to him and me. Later, he made sure that we got together. Who are we? *(Genesis 24)*

6. We were Bible "valentines" and God promised to give us children, even though we were very old. One of us laughed that we would ever get such a "valentine." Who are we? *(Genesis 17-21)*

7. Like the people in the last question, we were older "valentines" too, but one of us was speechless when God

told us of His promise that we would parent a prophet. Who are we? *(Luke 1)*

8. As "valentines" we were shirt-tail relation but we got together because of a famine, loyalty, and the barley harvest. Who are we? *(Ruth 4)*

9. One of us was a great king and because of the circumstances the other became his "valentine" queen and ended up rescuing God's people during a Persian persecution. Who are we? *(Esther 2)*

10. We were a "valentine" couple who were honored to have Jesus at our wedding and He provided a miraculous beverage to mark the occasion. Our names are not mentioned in the Bible but the place is. Name the place. *(John 2)*

11. We could be considered as being "evil valentines" because we plotted to get someone's land and stole it and also tried to destroy Elijah in a great "sacrifice contest" on Mt. Carmel. Who are we? *(I Kings 16-21)*

12. Our names are not "household names" but as husband and wife "valentines" we promised to do something special for God and then greedily changed our minds. We both died the same day. What are our names? *(Acts 5)*

13. Talk about a strange "valentine" encounter. We committed adultery, deceit and murder and then got married and were king and queen of Israel. No wonder God's prophet, Nathan, had to confront us. Who are we? *(II Samuel 11)*

14. My real "valentine" was Lapidoth but I worked with a man named Barak in leading the people through a time of unrest. What is my name? *(Judges 4)*

15. The name of my wife and "valentine" sweetheart are not mentioned in the Bible, but she looked back at the wrong time. Instead of candy, she turned into the "salt of the earth." What is my name. *(Genesis 19)*

ANSWERS: *(1) Adam and Eve, (2) Joseph and Mary, (3) Priscilla and Aquilla, (4) Jacob and Rachel, (5) Isaac and Rebekah, (6) Abraham and*

Pastor Willis Schwichtenberg

Sarah, (7) Zechariah and Elizabeth, (8) Ruth and Boaz, (9) Esther and Ahasuerus, (10) Cana, (11) Ahab and Jezebel, (12) Ananias and Sapphira, (13) David and Bathsheba, (14) Deborah, (15) Lot

SCORING: 15 or 14 correct—You are a sweetheart! 12-13 Correct—You love to study God's Word. 11-10 correct—Not bad; your days are sweet. 9-8 correct—You need to feel the love. 7 or Less Correct—Love is not in the air!

Veterans in the Bible

(Veteran's Day is November 11. Technically, the word "veteran" is not in the Bible but there are several soldiers mentioned. Try this Bible quiz to identify both positive and negative soldiers (and "veterans") in the pages of the Bible.)

1. As the first king of Israel I led the people against the Ammonites. I started well but later failed my Lord. Who am I? (I Samuel 10:20-24, 11:11) (a) Saul, (b) David, (c) Solomon, (d) Abner

2. I became a "soldier" in God's army when I agreed to face a giant man from Gath armed only with a sling, some stones, a smile and God's power. Who am I? (I Samuel 17:48-54) (a) Saul, (b) Jonathan, (c) David, (d) Solomon.

3. It was not a Veteran's Day observance but my name is David and at the death of the great soldier and king, Saul, I honored him and his son, Jonathan by saying (II Samuel 1:17-27) (a) Saul was swifter than eagles, (b) Saul was stronger than a lion, (c) "How the mighty have fallen," (d) "Don't publish this in Gath," (e) all of the above, (f) none of the above.

4. As a soldier commanding one hundred soldiers (a Centurion) I encountered Jesus and asked Him to heal my servant and I told Jesus (Matthew 8:5-13) (a) I was not worthy to have Him come to my house, (b) I asked Jesus to come to my house "today", (c) I was too shy to tell anyone what to do, (d) all of the above, (e) none of the above.

5. I was a soldier who heard John the Baptist talking to people about repentance and a changed life. Along with some other soldiers I asked him what I should do and he told us (Luke 3:14) (a) to give an offering, (b) to be

189

content with our wages, (c) to quit being soldiers and to follow Jesus, (d) to witness our faith to other soldiers.

6. I am Paul and I sent word to the Centurion in charge when I was arrested and I asked that I not be flogged because (Acts 22:22-26) (a) it hurt too much, (b) Jewish people were not to be flogged, (c) I was a Roman citizen, (d) I was innocent of any crime.

7. I was the governor and was very concerned about Paul and the people who were against him and had two Centurions enlist soldiers to protect him. This included (Acts 23:23) (a) 200 soldiers, (b) 70 horsemen, (c) 200 spearmen, (d) all of the above, (e) none of the above.

8. I am a Centurion soldier and I was very concerned about Paul and tried to help and protect him in his imprisonment as we battle the sea and shipwreck. What was my name? (Acts 27:1-2ff) (a) Julius, (b) Agrippa, (c) Festus, (d) Felix, (e) Claudius Lysias.

9. Sometimes soldiers have to wear armor. My name is Paul and I wrote about putting on the "whole armor of God" which included all of the following except (Ephesians 6:11-17) (a) belt of truth, (b) breastplate of righteousness, (c) glove to reach out to people, (d) shoes with the Gospel of peace, (e) shield of faith, (f) helmet of salvation, (g) sword of the Spirit.

10. My name is Paul and I called my co-worker Timothy a "good soldier" and told him to (II Timothy 2:3-4) (a) entrust the work to faithful men, (b) share in suffering, (c) not to get involved in civilian pursuits, (d) all of the above, (e) none of the above.

ANSWERS: *(1) a-Saul, (2) c-David, (3) e-all of the above, (4) a-I was not worthy to have Him come into my house, (5) b-to be content with our wages, (6) c-I was a Roman citizen, (7) d-all of the above, (8) a-Julius, (9) c-glove to reach out to people, (10) d-all of the above.*

SCORING: If you got all 10 correct, as a good soldier you have won the battle; if you got 9 correct you achieved near success as a solider; if you got 8 correct you need to restudy the battle plan; if you got 7 or fewer correct you need to ask yourself, "Is all lost?"

"Water in the Bible"

(When we move into the summer we consider the fact that sometimes our picnics and vacations are challenged by rain and water. Water is mentioned many times in the Bible. Using the clues given see if you can discover the rain or water reference being described. Check the Biblical reference if you need help.)

1. In the creation I was moving over the face of the water (Genesis 1-2) Who am I? (a) Jesus, (b) God the Father, (c) Dove, (d) Raven, (e) Spirit.

2. I told the people that I baptized with water for repentance (Matthew 3:1). Who am I? (a) Jesus, (b) John, (c) Peter, (d) John.

3. At the Pentecost celebration I quoted Scripture that living water would be flowing (John 7:38). Who am I? (a) Paul, (b) Peter, (c) John, (d) Jesus.

4. I humbly asserted that I planted and Apollos watered but God is the one who gives growth. (I Corinthians 3:6). Who am I? (a) Aquilla, (b) Priscilla, (c) Peter, (d) Paul, (e) none of the above.

5. I, Jesus, said that anyone who gives a little one a cup of cold water because of me would be one of these. (Matthew 10:42) What did I say that they would be? (a) a disciple, (b) an apostle, (c) a priest, (d) a servant, (e) a child of God.

6. I, James, wrote that a person who doubts is one of these (James 1:6). What was I referring to? (a) a drop in a puddle, (b) a wave in the sea, (c) a tree in a rainstorm, (d) sour water in a well.

7. In Psalm 22 I talked about being "poured out like water" as I felt abaondoned by God. (Psalm 22:14) My name is (a) Solomon, (b) Jesus, (c) David, (d) Korah, (e) Asaph.

8. In writing about marriage I, Paul, contrasted washing and cleaning with water (Ephesians 5:26) with (a) the Word, (b) the blood of Christ, (c) detergent, (d) fire.

9. According to Jeremiah 17:8 a tree planted by water (a) sends out its roots by the stream, (b) does not fear when heat comes, (c) does not cease to bear fruit, (d) all of the above.

10. Jesus asked me for a drink and used this encounter to talk about living water (John 4:7-15). Who am I? (a) Mary of Bethany, (b) the Woman of Samaria, (c) Mary Magdalene, (d) Salome, (e) Priscilla.

11. I was told by Elisha the Prophet to wash seven times in the Jordan River to cure my leprosy after I heard from my wife's Hebrew servant girl about his power. (II Kings 5:3-6, 14). Who am I? (a) Ahab, (b) Gehazi, (c) Naam (d) Moab, (e) Ben-Hadad.

12. Elisha and his prophets were building a new place to meet when a problem arose which caused Elisha to use water and a stick to perform a miracle. What was the miracle (II Kings 6:1-7)? (a) a dove returns with an olive branch in its beak, (b) an axe head floats on the water, (c) a rock is struck and it produces water, (d) Elisha walks on water, (e) the Red Sea is divided.

ANSWERS: (1) e/Spirit, (2) b/John, (3) d/Jesus, (4) d/Paul, (5) a/disciple, (6) b/wave in the sea, (7) c/David, (8) a/Word, (9)d/All of the above, (10) b/Woman of Samaria, (11) c/Naaman, (12) b/an axe head floats.

SCORING: 12 correct – You cleaned up; 10-11 correct – A cool and refreshing score!, 9 correct – it will all come out in the wash!, 8 or less – Try washing seven times!

Weather in the Bible

(According to Wikipedia, "Weather is the state of the atmosphere, to the degree that it is hot or cold, wet or dry, calm or stormy, clear or cloudy." That's a pretty bookish answer about the meaning of weather. I like Mark Twain's quotes about the weather. First, in a quote that many have adapted for their own use, Mark Twain said, "If you don't like the weather in New England, just wait a few minutes." He also may have been the first to say, "Everybody talks about the weather, but nobody does anything about it." A man named Jerome K. Jerome also wrote, "The weather is like the government, always in the wrong." The Bible has many references to the weather. Using the Biblical clues given, see if you can determine the thoughts about the weather which are described or the people involved in various Biblical weather situations. If you need help, you may wish to check the Bible passage.)

1. In my day rain fell on the earth 40 days and 40 nights. What's my name? (Genesis 7:12) (a) Noah, (b) Shem, (c) Adam, (d) John in Revelation, (e) Elijah.
2. I was the one who placed the bow or rainbow in the sky as a sign of the covenant between me and all humans in the world. Who am I? (Genesis 9:12-16) (a) Noah, (b) Abraham, (c) Isaac, (d) Jesus, (e) God.
3. My name is Moses and as part of a plague heavy hail fell from the sky, along with crashing thunder and unusual fire. Strangely enough, this "weather" did not take place in the land of God's people. Name this land. (Exodus 9:22-24) (a) Canaan, (b) Egypt, (c) Goshen, (d) Judah, (e) Israel.
4. My name is Joshua and it was a very unique thing that happened to the sun when our troops were facing an impossible enemy. Can you describe what happened? (Joshua 10:13) (a) a great flood came, (b) a famine

wracked the land, (c) the sun stood still, (d) there was snow in the summer.

5. My name is Gideon and when God was calling me to serve Him I asked that He would give me a sign. What was this "sign"? (Judges 6:36-40) (a) there would be dew on fleece but not on the ground, (b) there would be dew on the ground but not on the fleece, (c) all of the above, (d) none of the above.

6. We prayed for a special act in which our god would send down fire and consume our offering. We fervently prayed and cut ourselves, imploring for this "change" in weather. Who are we? (I Kings 18:26-29) (a) Elijah and his helpers, (b) the prophets of Baal, (c) Gideon and the Midianites, (d) the Philistines who opposed Samson.

7. In my day great strong winds tore a mountain in two and moved rocks. There was also an earthquake and fire. Who am I? (I Kings 19:11-12) (a) Elisha, (b) Moses, (c) Abraham, (d) Elijah, (e) Malachi

8. My name is Isaiah and under inspiration I wrote down words and thoughts of God about reasoning together. He guided me to write that "even though our sins were scarlet they would be as white" as something. What would they be as "white as"? (Isaiah 1:18) (a) fine linen, (b) snow, (c) the dew, (d) manna, (e) milk.

9. Jesus talked to the Pharisees and Sadducees and said that they were pretty good at predicting the weather. What did He tell them? (Matthew 16:1-4) (a) When it is evening and the sky is red you say it will be fair weather, (b) When it is morning and the sky is red you say it will be stormy, (c) all of the above, (d) none of the above.

10. In the days of Noah people did not pay much attention to the weather and many other things until "the flood came and swept them all away." What was the name of the man who gave this quote? (Matthew 24:39) (a) Jesus, (b) John the Baptist, (c) Elijah, (d) Herod.

11. My name is Jesus and during a boat ride with my disciples we faced a violent storm. Can you remember what happened in this storm? (Mark 4:35-40) (a) Jesus was asleep in the stern on a cushion, (b) the boat was filling with water, (c) The disciples said, "Do you not care that we are perishing?", (d) Jesus said to the sea, "Peace. Be still.", (e) all of the above.

12. My name is Jesus and it wasn't exactly the weather but this event happened as I hung on the cross dying in payment for sins but this unique weather was part of the day. (Luke 23:44) (a) No sun from the 6th to the 9th hour, (b) Pouring rain fell, (c) A violent windstorm destroyed the Temple, (d) Snow fell from the sky, (e) All of the above.

13. When I faced shipwreck on the way to Rome our ship faced a violet storm with no sun or stars visible for several days. Who am I? (Acts 27:18-20) (a) Simon Peter, (b) Apostle Paul, (c) Jonah, (d) Joseph of the Old Testament.

14. My name is James and in my epistle I talked about the great importance of prayer. I spoke of a man who prayed and there was no rain for 3 and a half years. Who was this man that I described? (James 5:17-18) (a) Noah, (b) Abraham, (c) Moses, (d) Elijah, (e) Job.

15. The weather described in an upheaval in the book of Revelation in chapter 16:21 was unique. What was unique about this weather? (a) the hail stones would weigh 100 pounds each, (b) a flood would drown the people like vermin, (c) fire would consume millions of people, (d) there would be a thousand year drought.

ANSWERS: *(1) a-Noah, (2) e-God, (3) c-Goshen, (4) c-the sun stood still, (5) c-all of the above, (6) b-the prophets of Baal, (7) d-Elijah, (8) b-snow, (9) c-all of the above, (10) a-Jesus, (11) e-all of the above, (12) a-No sun from the 6th to the 9th hour, (13) b-Apostle Paul, (14) d-Elijah, (15) a-the hail stones would weigh 100 pounds each.*

SCORING: 15-14 Correct-You are better than most weather predictors, 13-12 Correct-You could get a job on TV, 11-It will not rain on your parade, 10 or fewer correct-Again, you are better than most weather predictors!!!

Winter and Cold in the Bible

(We need no reminder of cold, snow, and the wintery weather that comes at the end of the year and in the early New Year. What does the Bible say about this? See if you can determine the weather related questions being described. Use the Biblical reference if you need help.)

1. After the flood God promised Noah and the people of the world that the following would never cease (Genesis 8:22): (a) seedtime and harvest, (b) cold and heat, (c) summer and winter, (d) day and night, (e) all of the "above".

2. When God was speaking to Moses about how he should lead the people Moses put his hand in his cloak and (Exodus 4:6) (a) found that it was white like snow when he pulled it out, (b) fiery red, (c) gnarled and shriveled, (d) none of the above.

3. The chilling affects of leprosy in causing skin to be "as white as snow" was not lost on Gehazi as he (II Kings 5:27) (a) was filled with fear and immediately died, (b) received the leprosy that was on Naaman for the rest of his life, (c) prayed and the leprosy was immediately removed, (d) became the famous "leprous prophet."

4. In Psalm 51 (verse 7) King David prays that he would be cleansed with hyssop and that when washed he would be (a) released by the rain and sleet, (b) restored from sickness, (c) whiter than snow, (d) forever forgiven.

5. God promises that the rain and the snow that come down from heaven (Isaiah 55:10) (a) do not return without watering the earth, (b) make the earth bud and flourish, (c) cause seed to come to the sower, (d) help to produce bread for the eater, (e) all of the above, (f) none of the above.

6. The prophet Daniel had a glimpse of God in heaven and saw that (Daniel 7:9) (a) His clothing was as white as

snow, (b) the hair on His head was white like wool, (c) His throne was flaming with fire, (d) He had wheels which were blazing, (e) all of the above.

7. Jesus talked about not "losing our reward" when we are able to give this to someone (Matthew 10:42): (a) a snowball, (b) shelter for the winter, (c) a cup of cold water, (d) flakes of new fallen snow.

8. Jesus has a major confrontation about His divinity with the rulers and religious leaders of the people in the winter at the following "feast" (John 10:22): (a) Passover, (b) Hanukkah, (c) Day of Atonement, (d) Unleavened Bread, (e) Dedication.

9. Toward the end of his earthly life in His discourses Jesus warned that because of the increase of wickedness the following would happen (Matthew 24:12): (a) love of most would grow cold, (b) the earth would enter an ice age, (c) the earth would become hot, (d) attitudes would "simmer", (e) none of the above.

10. In warning of the end times Jesus says that we should pray (Matthew 24:20) (a) it would not take place in winter, (b) that snow would fall to quench the heat, (c) that sleet and rain would cool the earth, (d) that God would protect us with holy snow.

11. When the Apostle Peter was confronted by the soldiers after the arrest of Jesus people were (John 18:18): (a) shoveling snow in the entryway, (b) chipping ice off the stones, (c) standing around a fire because it was cold, (d) sheltering themselves from the rain which was falling.

12. The clothes of this person at the Tomb on Easter Sunday was as "white as snow" (Matthew 28:3): (a) Mary Magdalene, (b) Jesus Christ, (c) Simon Peter, (d) Apostle John, (e) Angel.

13. In his account in the book of Acts (Acts 28:2) the writer Luke talks about the people on the island of Malta (a) staying indoors because of the cold, (b) building a fire

because of the rain and cold, (c) swimming in the cold water, (d) using chunks of coal for a brazier.

14. In his writings to the Corinthians the Apostle Paul says that he (II Corinthians 11:27) (a) often went without sleep, (b) knew hunger and thirst, (c) often went without food, (d) had often been cold and naked, (e) all of the above, (f) none of the above.

15. To the Laodicean church God spoke and said that they were (Revelation 3:15-16) (a) greasy and curdled, (b) steamy and sweaty, (c) neither hot nor cold, (d) frigid like ice, (e) hot like peppers.

16. In writing to Timothy Paul tells him that he hopes to see him before (II Timothy 4:21) (a) the fall rain, (b) the snow showers, (c) the winter, (d) the spring.

<ANSWERS: (1) e/all of the above; (2) a/found that it was white as snow; (3) b/received the leprosy that was on Naaman; (4) c/whiter than snow; (5) e/all of the above; (6) e/all of the above; (7) c/a cup of cold water; (8) e/ Dedication; (9) a/love of most would grow cold; (10) a/it would not take place in winter; (11) c/standing around a fire because it was cold; (12) e/ Angel; (13) b/building a fire because of the rain and cold; (14) e/all of the above; (15) c/neither hot nor cold; (16) c/the winter.

SCORING: 16 or 15 correct – You have the warmth and comfort of knowing God's Word, 14 or 13 correct – You are neither hot nor cold; 12 or 11 correct – Things are a bit chilly but study of God's Word will warm you up; 10 or less correct – You need to get closer to the fire!

Writing in the Bible

(When we think about school we think about reading, writing, and arithmetic. When it comes to writing, we believe that the Bible is the written Word of God. Many Biblical authors were told to write down God's Word and share it with others. Using the clues given see if you can discover the Biblical writer or writing being described. Check the Biblical reference if you need help. If the book reference gives away the name of the writer, the book reference is not given.)

1. I was the first human Biblical writer and was told by God to write things down. What is my name? (Exodus 24:4) (a) Moses, (b) Aaron, (c) Jeremiah, (d) Noah.

2. My name is Jeremiah and I had an assistant who wrote down my prophecies. What was his name? (Jeremiah 36:4) (a) Barack, (b) Isaiah, (c) Nebuchadnezzar, (d) Baruch

3. I was told to eat a scroll in the Old Testament. Who am I? (3:1-3). (a) Baruch, (b) Jeremiah, (c) Ezekiel, (d) Jonah.

4. I wrote my "Ten Words" for Moses with my finger. Who am I? (Exodus 20) (a) Aaron, (b) Korah, (c) God, (d) Joshua.

5. I signed one of my New Testament letters with big bold letters, a quirk that makes some people suggest I had eyesight problems. Who am I? (Galatians 6:11) (a) Timothy, (b) Paul, (c) Titus, (d) James.

6. I wrote to Theophilis about information about Jesus. My name is not directly given but is implied from history and tradition. Who am I? (Luke 1:1-4, Acts 1:1-4) (a) Paul, (b) Apollos, (c) Luke, (d) John.

7. I led a major church assembly in which we ended up writing a letter to Gentile Christians. Who am I? (Acts 15:12ff.) (a) James, (b) Paul, (c) Barnabas, (d) Mark.

8. God told me to write down letters to seven churches in Asia Minor. Who am I? (Revelation 1:1-5) (a) Gabriel, (b) Michael, (c) Paul, (d) John

9. I was a pagan ruler who wrote a decree that the Babylonian exiles could return home. Who am I? (II Chronicles 36:22-23) (a) Nebuchadnezzar, (b) Belshazzar, (c) Cyrus, (d) Antiochus Epiphanes.

10. I wrote that some of Paul's letters were difficult to understand. Who am I? (II Peter 3:15-16) (a) Apollos, (b) John, (c) James, (d) Simon Peter.

11. I compiled many of the Old Testament Scriptures after the Babylonian exile. I also assisted Nehemiah with his work of leading the people. Who am I? (Nehemiah 8:1ff.) (a) Ezra, (b) Amminidab, (c) Joshua, (d) Uriah the Hittite

12. I decreed that words about Jesus should be placed above his head on the cross, to the objection of some. Who am I? (John 19:19-22) (a) Herod, (b) Caiaphas, (c) Annas, (d) Pontius Pilate

ANSWERS: *(1) a/Moses; (2) d/Baruch, (3) c/Ezekiel; (4) c/God; (5) b/ Paul; (6) c/Luke; (7) a/James; (8) d/John; (9) c/Cyrus; (10) d/Simon Peter; (11) a/Ezra; (12) d/Pontius Pilate.*

SCORING: 12 correct – You are all right/write!; 11 or 10 correct – You demonstrate that the pen is mightier than the sword; 9 correct – Enter your score in your journal because it's pretty good; 8 or less correct – Not bad, but it's really nothing to write home about!

Printed in the United States
by Baker & Taylor Publisher Services